MW00574417

Exploration, Revolution, and Constitution

American History Series

Author: Cindy Barden

Consultants: Schyrlet Cameron and Suzanne Myers

Editors: Mary Dieterich and Sarah M. Anderson

Proofreader: Margaret Brown

COPYRIGHT © 2011 Mark Twain Media, Inc.

ISBN 978-1-58037-582-5

Printing No. CD-404137

Mark Twain Media, Inc., Publishers
Distributed by Carson-Dellosa Publishing LLC

Visit us at www.carsondellosa.com

Table of Contents

Table of Contents (cont.)

About the American History Series

Exploration, Revolution, and Constitution is one of the books in Mark Twain Media's new *American History Series.* This book focuses on the early history of America, from the Age of Discovery to the birth of the new nation. Students will learn about the voyages of the European explorers, everyday life in the American colonies, the struggle for freedom during the American Revolution, and the compromises made in forming the American government. This series is

designed to provide students in grades 5 through 8 with opportunities to explore the significant events and people that make up American history. Other books in the series include *Westward Expansion and Migration; Slavery, Civil War, and Reconstruction;* and *Industrialization Through the Great Depression.*

The books in this series are written for classroom teachers, parents, and students. They are designed as stand-alone material for classrooms and home schooling. Also, the books can be used as supplemental material to enhance the history curriculum in the classroom, independent study, or as a tutorial at home.

The text in each book is presented in an easy-to-read format that does not overwhelm the struggling reader. Vocabulary words are boldfaced. Each book provides challenging activities that enable students to explore history, geography, and social studies topics. The activities promote reading, critical thinking, and writing skills. As students learn about the people who influenced history, they will draw conclusions; write opinions; compare and contrast historical events, people, and places; analyze cause and effect; and improve mapping skills. The research and technology activities will further increase their knowledge and understanding of historical events by using the reference sources of the Internet.

The easy-to-follow format of the books facilitates planning for the diverse learning styles and skill levels of middle-school students. National standards addressed in each unit are identified and listed at the beginning of the book, simplifying lesson preparation. Each unit provides the teacher with alternative methods of instruction: reading exercises for concept development, simple hands-on activities to strengthen understanding of concepts, and challenging investigations using technology in the classroom to provide opportunities for students to expand learning. A bibliography of suggested resources is included to assist the teacher in finding additional resources or to provide a list of recommended reading for students who want to expand their knowledge.

The *American History Series* supports the No Child Left Behind (NCLB) Act. The books promote student knowledge and understanding of history concepts. The content and activities are designed to strengthen the understanding of historical events that have shaped our nation. The units are correlated with the National Standards for United States History (NSH) and Curriculum Standards for Social Studies (NCSS).

Unit Planning Guide

National Standards Matrix

Each unit of study in the book *Exploration, Revolution, and Constitution* is designed to strengthen American history literacy skills and is correlated with the National History Standards (NHS) and Curriculum Standards for Social Studies (NCSS).

National History Standards	Unit 1	Unit 2	Unit 3
Standard 1: Chronological Thinking	x	x	x
Standard 2: Historical Comprehension	x	x	x
Standard 3: Historical Analysis and Interpretation	x	x	x
Standard 4. Historical Research Capablities	x	x	x
Curriculum Standards for Social Studies			
Standard 1: Culture	x	x	x
Standard 2: Time, Continuity, and Change	x	x	x
Standard 3: People, Places, and Environments	x	x	x
Standard 4: Individual Development and Identity	x	x	x
Standard 5: Individuals, Groups, and Institutions	x	x	x
Standard 6: Power, Authority, and Governance	x		x
Standard 7: Production, Distribution, and Consumption	x	x	x
Standard 8: Science, Technology, and Society		x	
Standard 9: Global Connections	x		x
Standard 10: Civil Ideals and Practices	x		x

Suggested Resources

Arnold, James R. *The Revolutionary War* series. New York: Grolier. 2004.

Aronson, Marc. *The World Made New: Why the Age of Exploration Happened & How It Changed the World.* Des Moines, Iowa: National Geographic Children's Books. 2007.

Berger, Melvin. *The Real Vikings: Craftsmen, Traders, and Fearsome Raiders.* Des Moines, Iowa: National Geographic Children's Books. 2004.

Bobrick, Bensen. *Fight for Freedom: The American Revolutionary War.* New York: Scholastic. 2007.

Bohannon, Lisa Frederiksen. *The American Revolution.* Minneapolis, Minnesota: Lerner Publishing Group. 2003.

Cameron, Schyrlet, Janie Doss and Suzanne Myers. *Using Primary Sources in the Social Studies and Language Arts Classroom.* Quincy, Illinois: Mark Twain Media, Inc. 2006.

Carlson, Laurie M. *Colonial Kids: An Activity Guide to Life in the New World.* Chicago: Chicago Review Press. 1997.

Doherty, Craig A. and Katherine M. Doherty. *Thirteen Colonies* series. New York: Facts on File. 2005.

Fleming, Thomas. *Everybody's Revolution: A New Look at the People Who Won America's Freedom.* New York: Scholastic Nonfiction. 2006.

Freedman, Russell. *Who Was First? Discovering the Americas.* New York: Clarion. 2007.

Herbert, Janis. *The American Revolution for Kids.* Chicago: Chicago Review Press, Inc. 2002.

Kalman, Bobbie, Niki Walker, et al. *Colonial People* series. New York: Crabtree. 2002.

McNeese, Tim. *The Fascinating History of American Indians: The Age Before Columbus.* Berkeley Heights, New Jersey: Enslow Publishing. 2009.

Micklos, John Jr. *The Revolutionary War Library* series. Berkeley Heights, New Jersey: Enslow Publishing. 2009.

Miller, Brandon Marie. *Declaring Independence: Life During the American Revolution.* Minneapolis, Minnesota: Lerner Publishing Group. 2005.

Miller, Brandon Marie. *Good Women of a Well-Blessed Land: Women's Lives in Colonial America.* Minneapolis, Minnesota: Lerner Publishing Group. 2003.

Miller, Jake, Melody S. Mis, et al. *Primary Sources of the Thirteen Colonies* series. New York: Rosen Publishing Group, Inc. 2006.

Murray, Stuart. *American Revolution.* New York: DK Children. 2002.

Sanders, Nancy I. *America's Black Founders: Revolutionary Heroes and Early Leaders: With 21 Activities.* Chicago: Chicago Review Press, Inc. 2010.

Schomp, Virginia. *The Vikings.* Danbury, Conneticut: Children's Press. 2005.

Smith, Tom. *Discovery of the Americas, 1492–1800.* New York: Facts on File. 2005.

Wyatt, Valerie. *Who Discovered America?* Tonawanda, New York: Kids Can Press, Ltd. 2008.

Time Line for Discovering and Exploring the Americas

30,000 B.C. –	
4,000 B.C.	Migrations across the Bering Strait to Alaska
about 985 A.D.	Erik the Red discovered Greenland
about 1000	Leif Erikson arrived in North America
1492 – 1502	Columbus made four voyages to the New World
1493	Ponce de León arrived in Santo Domingo
1496	John Cabot's first unsuccessful voyage
1497	John Cabot landed in Newfoundland
1497 – 1499	Vasco da Gama discovered a sea route around Africa to India
1498	John Cabot, four ships, and crew lost at sea
1499 – 1512	Amerigo Vespucci explored coast of South America
1501	Vasco de Balboa arrived in South America
1508	Sebastian Cabot explored Hudson Bay
1509	Ponce de León appointed Governor of Puerto Rico
1513	Vasco de Balboa first saw the Pacific Ocean
1513	Ponce de León searched for the fountain of youth
1519	Hernan Cortés founded Veracruz
1520	Ferdinand Magellan sailed from Spain, around South America, to India
1521	Hernan Cortés conquered the Aztec Empire in Mexico
1524	Hernan Cortés led an expedition to Honduras
1526	Sebastian Cabot set off on a four-year voyage
1530	Francisco Pizarro conquered the Incas of Peru
1534 – 1541	Jacques Cartier made three voyages to Newfoundland
1536	Hernan Cortés discovered Baja California
1537	Hernando de Soto appointed Governor of Florida
1538	Francisco de Coronado appointed Governor of New Galicia
1539 – 1542	Hernando de Soto explored southeastern United States
1540 – 1541	Francisco de Coronado searched for the Seven Cities of Cíbola
1541	Hernando de Soto first saw the Mississippi River
1607 – 1608	Henry Hudson searched for a shortcut to India for the Muscovy Company
1608	Samuel de Champlain helped found Quebec
1609	Henry Hudson explored the Hudson River for the Dutch East India Company, giving the Netherlands claim to land around New York
1611	Henry Hudson set adrift in Hudson Bay by mutineers
1633	Samuel de Champlain became Governor of New France
1682	Robert La Salle explored the Mississippi River to the Gulf of Mexico
1684	Robert La Salle sent to establish a French colony at the mouth of the Mississippi River

Name: _____   Date: _____

Discovering and Exploring the Americas
Time Line Activity

Use information from the time line to fill in the blanks.

1. What year did Hernado de Soto first see the Mississippi River? _____

2. In 1513, for what was Ponce de León searching? _____

3. In what year did John Cabot have his first unsuccessful voyage? _____

4. In what year did Erik the Red discover Greenland? _____

5. In 1524, where did Hernan Cortés lead an expedition? _____

6. Who founded Veracruz? _____

7. Where did Robert La Salle explore in 1682? _____

8. In what year did Sebastian Cabot set off on a four-year voyage? _____

9. Who arrived in South America in 1501? _____

10. Approximately when did Leif Erikson arrive in North America? _____

11. In what year did Vasco de Balboa first see the Pacific Ocean? _____

12. In what year did Francisco Pizarro conquer the Incas of Peru? _____

13. Who explored the Hudson Bay in 1508? _____

14. During what time span did Amerigo Vespucci explore the coast of South America?

    _____

15. In what year did Hernan Cortés discover Baja California? _____

16. Where did Hernado de Soto explore from 1539 to 1542? _____

17. Where was Henry Hudson set adrift by mutineers in 1611? _____

18. During what time span did Christopher Columbus make four voyages to the New World?

    _____

19. In 1608, who helped found Quebec? _____

20. In what year did John Cabot land in Newfoundland? _____

Land Bridge Theory

The first people to discover the New World weren't famous Europeans. They weren't sailors or explorers searching for a new world. Who were they? How did they get to the Americas? From where did they come? Why did they come? When did they arrive?

Although the names of those who first journeyed to North America are not recorded, we do know a little about them and how they traveled. The first people to arrive in the Americas didn't sail here in large ships. They walked thousands of miles across Siberia to Alaska. During the ice ages, a land bridge connected the two continents.

Small groups of **nomads** began arriving in North America about 30,000 years ago. As they traveled, **migrating** groups might settle for a time in a place that offered good hunting or fishing. Some stayed for a year or two or even many, many years before moving on. Eventually, some of the group or their **descendents** continued the journey, following the migrating herds of animals they hunted.

Today, only about 80 miles separate Siberia and Alaska.

Not all groups made the journey at the same time. Many waves of migrants crossed the Siberian land bridge during a period covering more than 25,000 years. The last migration occurred about 4,000 years ago.

By the time Christopher Columbus set sail from Spain in 1492, thousands of groups of people with many different cultures and languages lived in the Americas.

UNIT ONE: EXPLORATION

Matching

_____ 1. explorer

_____ 2. descendents

_____ 3. migrate

_____ 4. nomads

a. people who are offspring, however remote, of a certain ancestor, family, or group

b. moving from one place to another; to move from one region to another with the change in seasons

c. one who travels in an unknown or little-known region

d. a tribe or people having no permanent home, but moving about constantly in search of food, pasture, etc.

Name: _____ Date: _____

Viking Exploration

Although we usually think of Christopher Columbus as being the first European to visit the Americas, evidence suggests that by the time Columbus set sail, the voyages of the first Europeans to the New World had been long forgotten. Norsemen (Vikings from Scandinavia) sailed from Greenland to Newfoundland, where they set up a colony about 500 years before Columbus was even born. Where they landed and built settlements is uncertain. Viking ruins found in northern Newfoundland, a province of Canada, suggest that at least one settlement was in that area. Some, like Erik the Red, settled in Iceland and later in Greenland.

Stories of the life and adventures of Erik the Red, Leif the Lucky, and other Viking explorers were handed down orally for about 200 years before being written. The original documents have been lost, and only copies written in the 1300s and 1400s remain. Europeans who read about the adventures of the Vikings may have believed they were only made-up stories.

In 1964, President Lyndon B. Johnson and Congress officially recognized Leif Erikson as the first European to land in North America by proclaiming October 9 as "Leif Erikson Day."

 Technology in the Classroom

Mini CyberHunt

Directions: To learn more about Viking exploration, use the following Internet websites to find the answers to the CyberHunt questions. Answers should be written on your own paper.

1. How is Old Norse religion similar to the religion of the Ancient Egyptians? (Hint: Go to Homeland/Archaeology)
   <http://www.mnh.si.edu/vikings/start.html>

2. What was the common size of a crew on a Viking longship?
   <http://www.bbc.co.uk/history/ancient/vikings/weapons_01.shtml>

3. What are runes?
   <http://www.pbs.org/wgbh/nova/vikings/runes.html>

4. One of the favorite toys of the Vikings was a board game called _____.
   <http://www.bbc.co.uk/schools/primaryhistory/vikings/family_life/>

5. There were two types of Viking ships, the longship and the _____.
   <http://ww2.mariner.org/exploration/index.php?type=shiptype&id=20>

Leif the Lucky

Born: sometime after A.D. 960 in Iceland
Died: sometime before 1025, probably in Greenland

Born in Iceland, Leif Erikson was one of three sons of Erik the Red, a man who moved from Norway to Iceland when he was young. About 985 A.D., Erik got into trouble and was **banished** from Iceland for three years. He and a small crew set off to explore the area west of Iceland. It is uncertain whether Leif went with his father, but he probably did because that was the usual custom at the time.

When he returned, Erik reported that he had found a new land with green fields that he named Greenland. He convinced others to move with him and his family to the new land.

Erik the Red became one of Greenland's leaders. He sent Leif on a ship to Norway in 997 A.D. to take presents to King Olaf and to trade furs, walrus and narwhal ivory, **woolens**, live polar bears, and **gyrfalcons** for items the colonists needed, like iron, timber, and grains. The king commanded Leif to take the teachings of Christianity back to his people. Evidence of a small church has been found near the area where Erik the Red and his family lived in Greenland.

As the colony in Greenland grew larger, they had one serious problem—lack of trees for building ships and homes. The few trees that grew there were small and scrubby. Leif had heard stories of other lands beyond Greenland, lands with many large trees. Around the year 1000 A.D., Leif sailed in search of those lands.

The first place Leif and his crew landed was probably Baffin Island. Leif named it

Most details about Leif Erikson's life and explorations have been lost. Even his name is not certain. Some sources use the spelling Liev, others, Leif. His last name, meaning "son of Erik", has been spelled Ericson, Eriksson, Erickson, and Erikson.

Helluland. Sailing southwest, they sighted Markland, which was probably the coast of Labrador. Finally they came to a channel that led to a river. They saw large salmon in the water, seabirds in the air, plants, trees, and evidence of animals on land. They called it Vinland—**"Land of Meadows"**—and spent the winter there. It could have been in northern Newfoundland or as far south as Cape Cod, Massachusetts.

On their **voyage** home the following spring, Leif and his crew rescued sailors who had been shipwrecked on an island off the coast of Greenland. Because of this event and his discovery of Vinland, he was nicknamed Leif the Lucky.

Leif never returned to the land he had discovered. His father died, and Leif took his place as leader of the settlement in Greenland.

Name: _____   Date: _____

Leif the Lucky (cont.)

Directions: Complete the following activities.

Matching

_____   1. banished   a. arctic falcon

_____   2. woolens   b. Vinland

_____   3. gyrfalcons   c. enforced removal

_____   4. Land of Meadows   d. journey or travel by sea

_____   5. voyage   e. garments made of wool fabric

Fill in the Blanks

1. Leif Erikson was one of _____ sons of Erik the _____.

2. Erik the Red became one of _____ leaders.

3. King Olaf commanded Leif to take the teachings of _____ back to his

    people.

4. As the colony in Greenland grew larger, they had one serious problem—_____

    of _____ for building ships and homes.

5. Because he was able to rescue some shipwrecked sailors and his discovery of Vinland,

    he was nicknamed _____ the _____.

Critical Thinking

Considering all that happened to him, do you think Leif the Lucky was an appropriate nickname?
Why or why not? Give specific details to support your opinion.

_____

_____

_____

_____

_____

_____

_____

Name: _____ Date: _____

The Lands of the Vikings

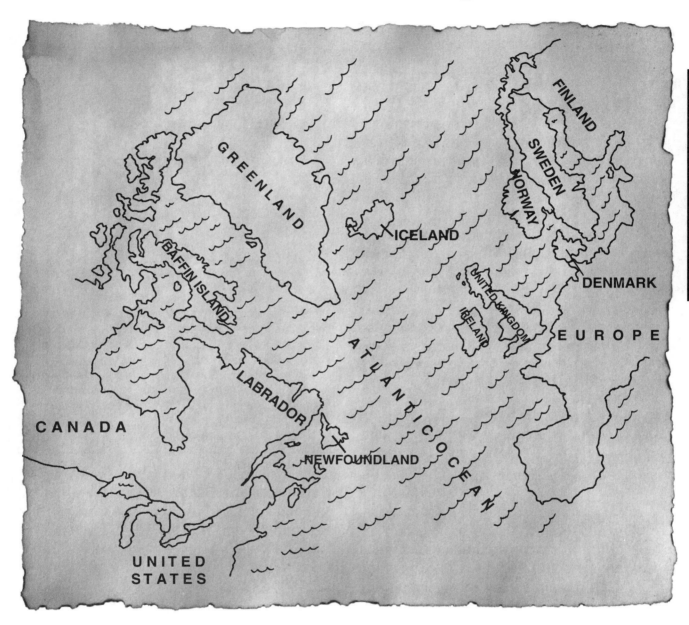

1. Use blue to color Iceland, the land where Erik the Red lived before he was banished for three years.
2. Use green to color Greenland, the land discovered by Erik the Red.
3. Use brown to color Norway, the country where King Olaf ruled.
4. Use red to circle Baffin Island, the island Leif the Lucky named Helluland.
5. Use orange to circle the coast of Labrador, the place Leif the Lucky called Markland.
6. Use yellow to circle Newfoundland.

Christopher Columbus

Born: in Genoa, Italy, in 1451
Died: 1506

In 1476, Christopher Columbus made his first trading voyage on the Atlantic Ocean. During this voyage, while sailing off the coast of Portugal, the **fleet** of ships was attacked by French **privateers**, or pirates. The ship that Columbus was on burned, and he had to swim for shore.

Later, Columbus would join several voyages to Africa. From these expeditions, he learned about the currents in the Atlantic Ocean.

In 1485, Columbus asked the Portuguese king, John II, to **finance** a voyage that would try to discover a western route to Asia. The king rejected his plan.

In 1486, he began petitioning King Ferdinand II and Queen Isabella of Spain for their financial support. It wasn't until 1492 that he finally gained their approval.

When he sailed from Spain in 1492, Christopher Columbus was not looking for a new world. Although Columbus and many others believed the earth was round, they simply didn't realize how large it actually was.

Columbus set sail looking for an ocean route to Asia that would be shorter and safer than traveling by land. If indeed the earth was round, it made sense to sail west to reach the lands of the east. Little did anyone realize that a huge landmass, the **continents** of North and South America, lay between Europe and Asia.

The person we know as Christopher Columbus was never known by that name while he was alive. He himself used several names to fit the country in which he lived. In Italy, his name was **Cristoforo Colombo**; in Portugal, he became **Cristavao Colom**. To the Spanish, he was **Cristobal Colon**; to the French, he was **Christophe Colombe**. The Latinized version of his name came to be used by English historians. To us, the man will always be **Christopher Columbus**.

Columbus landed in the Caribbean on an island in the Bahamas, which he named San Salvador. Thinking he had reached the East Indies and had found a new route to Asia, he called the people who lived there Indians. He sailed on to the islands of Cuba and Hispaniola. Off the coast of Hispaniola, the *Santa Maria,* the largest ship, wrecked. The other two ships, the *Niña,* and the *Pinta*, returned to Spain.

Christopher Columbus made three more voyages to the **New World**. When he died in 1506, he still thought he had found the water route to Asia.

Name: _____   Date: _____

Christopher Columbus (cont.)

Directions: Complete the following activities.

Matching

_____ 1. fleet
_____ 2. privateers
_____ 3. finance
_____ 4. continents

_____ 5. New World

a. provide funds or money
b. a large formation of ships
c. legalized pirates
d. landmasses in the Western Hemisphere
e. seven large landmasses

Fill in the Blanks

1. In 1476, Christopher Columbus made his first trading voyage on the _____ _____.

2. In 1486, he began petitioning King _____ II and Queen _____ of _____ for their financial support.

3. Columbus set sail looking for an ocean route to _____ that would be shorter and safer than traveling by _____.

4. Columbus landed in the Caribbean on an island in the Bahamas, which he named _____ _____.

5. Thinking he had reached the _____ _____ and had found a new route to Asia, he called the people who lived there _____.

Constructed Response

Explain why Christopher Columbus searched for a western route to Asia. Give specific details to support your answer.

_____

_____

_____

_____

_____

_____

Name: _____   Date: _____

The Four Voyages of Columbus

Directions: Use the map to complete the activity below.

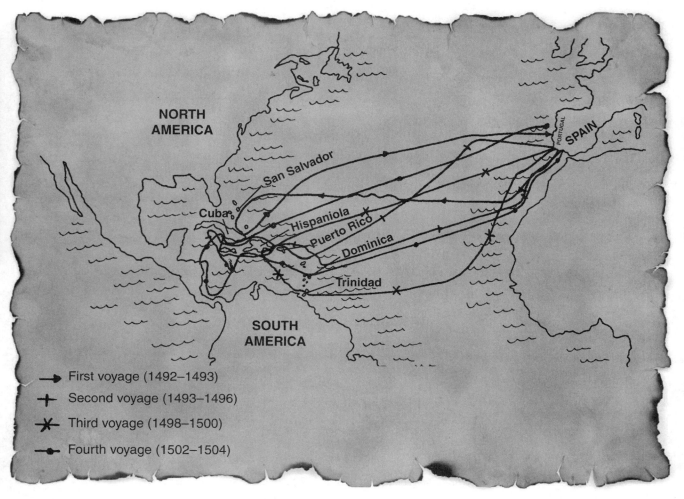

1.   Trace the first voyage of Columbus in red.

2.   Trace the second voyage of Columbus in green.

3.   Trace the third voyage of Columbus in blue.

4.   Trace the fourth voyage of Columbus in orange.

5.   Color Spain brown.

6.   Circle San Salvador in purple.

7.   Label the Atlantic Ocean.

Vasco Núñez de Balboa

Born: around 1475 in Jerez de los Caballeros, Spain
Died: 1519

Vasco Núñez de Balboa made his first voyage to the New World in 1501 with Don Rodrigo de Bastidas, a wealthy Spanish nobleman. After exploring the coast of Venezuela and trading with Native Americans, they wanted to return to Spain. Their ships were in bad shape, and they made it only as far as the island of Hispaniola before sinking near shore. Eventually Bastidas returned to Spain, but Balboa stayed in Hispaniola where he became a planter. Seven years later his **plantation** had failed, and he was deeply in debt.

Considered the first of the Spanish conquistadors (leaders of the Spanish conquest in the New World), Balboa is remembered for being the first European to see the Pacific Ocean.

> **Did You Know?**
> Hispaniola is the second largest island of the West Indies. It is divided into Haiti and the Dominican Republic.

In 1510, anxious to escape his **creditors**, Balboa convinced a friend to help him hide in a barrel and smuggle him aboard a ship. When discovered, the captain threatened to have Balboa **marooned** on a deserted island. Luckily, he changed his mind and allowed Balboa to become one of the crew. The captain and his crew built a settlement and named it San Sebastian.

At San Sebastian, men fell ill from lack of food and snake and insect bites. Native Americans attacked frequently with poison-tipped arrows and eventually burned the settlement to the ground.

Balboa suggested the survivors move to the settlement of Darien on the **Isthmus** of Panama. After a time, Balboa was elected as leader of the town. Food was plentiful in the area and so was gold. Balboa and his men learned to eat new foods including potatoes, corn, and pineapples—crops that did not grow in Europe at that time.

Balboa and his men explored the inland areas of Panama and brought Native Americans under Spanish rule. Unlike later **conquistadors**, Balboa used **diplomacy** instead of force. He believed it was better to have the native people as friendly neighbors rather than bitter enemies, a lesson many other Spanish leaders never learned.

When the man who had been appointed governor of Darien arrived, Balboa and the other settlers forced him to leave. They believed he would take away everything they had worked to earn.

Although no one else was blamed, Balboa was accused of treason in 1513. Hoping

UNIT ONE: EXPLORATION

Vasco Núñez de Balboa (cont.)

to win back the favor of King Ferdinand, he began searching for the great sea and fabulous cities of gold rumored to be on the other side of the isthmus. Although Balboa found some gold, the fabulous cities he heard about were those of the Incas of Peru, who were later conquered and destroyed by Francisco Pizarro.

Balboa led 190 Spanish soldiers and 800 Native Americans across the thick swamps and jungles of Panama. To find the way, he hired guides who took them as far as they could, and then he sent them back with rewards and hired others to continue. On September 29, 1513, they reached the Pacific Ocean. Balboa named it Mar del Sur (South Sea) and claimed it for Spain.

Balboa sent word of his discovery to the king, plus gifts of gold and pearls, but the king had already sent a new governor, Pedrarias, to Darien.

This is part of a letter from King Ferdinand to Balboa.

> ... I was rejoiced to read your letters and to learn of the things you discovered ... you will be honored and your services **recompensed** ... I am pleased with the way you behaved to the chiefs on that march, with kindness and **forbearance** ... When your letters came, Pedrarias had already left. I am writing to him to look to your affairs with care and to favor you as a person whom I greatly desire to gratify and who has greatly served me, and I am sure that he will do so.

Although Balboa had regained the king's favor, been given the title admiral, and named governor of the South Sea, Panama, and Coiba, the king had left it up to Pedrarias to give Balboa permission for any undertaking. Pedrarias was greedy and jealous of Balboa's success. He sent his soldiers to torture the natives and steal their gold.

Disturbed at the treatment of people who had become his friends, Balboa decided to leave Darien in 1515. Pedrarias refused to give his permission, but Balboa left anyway. He and 200 men traveled to a village of friendly Indians to prepare for another journey to the Pacific Ocean and a trip to Peru.

After King Ferdinand died, Pedrarias feared that he would be recalled to Spain and punished for his cruel treatment of the natives. To draw attention away from his own misdeeds, he sent Francisco Pizarro to escort Balboa to Acla where he was arrested, convicted of treason, and beheaded.

Before his death, Balboa had recommended that a channel be cut through the isthmus to connect the Atlantic and Pacific Oceans. However, that plan wasn't carried out for more than 400 years, when the Panama Canal was built by the United States.

Panama has honored Balboa by naming its monetary unit, the balboa, after him.

Vasco Núñez de Balboa (cont.)

Directions: Complete the following activities.

Matching

_____ 1. plantation
_____ 2. creditor
_____ 3. marooned
_____ 4. isthmus
_____ 5. conquistador
_____ 6. diplomacy
_____ 7. recompensed
_____ 8. forbearance

a. patience
b. someone to whom a debt is owed
c. one who conquers other people
d. reimbursed or rewarded
e. narrow strip of land connecting two land areas
f. large farm or estate
g. the practice of conducting negotiations between nations
h. to be stranded or left behind

Fill in the Blanks

1. Vasco Núñez de Balboa made his first voyage to the _____ _____ in 1501.

2. At the settlement of Darien, food was plentiful in the area and so was _____.

3. Balboa and his men explored the inland areas of _____ and brought Native Americans under Spanish rule.

4. Balboa led 190 Spanish soldiers and 800 _____ _____ across the thick swamps and jungles of Panama.

5. On September 29, 1513, they reached the _____ _____ and Balboa named it Mar de Sur (South Sea).

Constructed Response

Balboa used diplomacy instead of force with the Native Americans. Why? Support your answer with details or examples.

_____

_____

_____

_____

_____

Name: _____ Date: _____

Trade With the Far East

By the mid-14th century, trade had been established between Europe, China, and other countries in Asia. People were willing to pay large amounts of money for the rich silks, exotic spices, and other luxury items from Asia. But the overland route to Asia was long and dangerous. Much of the route was controlled by the Ottoman Turks, who were not friendly to Europeans. A route to Asia around the tip of Africa was not discovered until 1498 by Vasco da Gama.

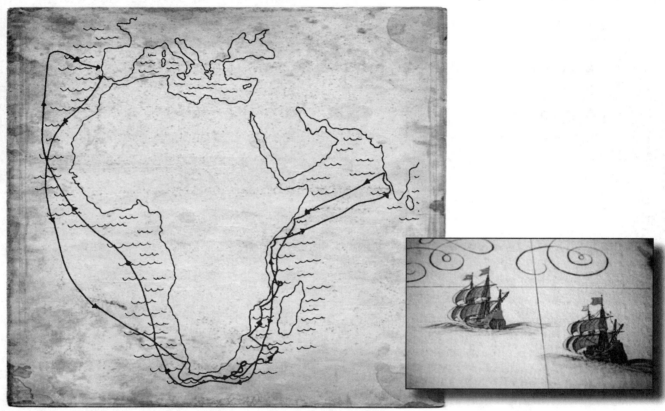

Research

Directions: Use the Internet or other reference sources and the map above to answer the following questions.

1. What continent did Vasco da Gama sail around to reach India? _____

2. What did da Gama hope to accomplish by his voyage? _____
   _____

3. What, if any, obstacles did he have to overcome on the voyage? _____
   _____

4. How long was the voyage? _____

5. What were the accomplishments of his voyage? _____
   _____

Amerigo Vespucci

Born: 1454 in Florence, Italy
Died: 1512

Since people believed Christopher Columbus was the first European to visit the New World, why weren't the continents named North and South Columbia? Columbus never realized he discovered a New World. When he died, he still thought he had found a sea route to the East Indies.

Like Columbus, Amerigo Vespucci was Italian. As a young man, he had an interest in mathematics, **cartography**, and **astronomy**. He worked for bankers in Florence, Italy, and was sent to Spain to look after the bank's business there. While in Spain, he made his first voyage, not as the captain, but as a **navigator**.

In 1499, the crew explored the coast of South America to the mouth of the Amazon River. By observing the conjunction of Mars and the moon, Vespucci was able to calculate how far west he had traveled.

Vespucci's second voyage in 1501 was on a Portuguese ship. The voyage across the Atlantic Ocean took 64 days. Again the crew explored the coast of South America to within 400 miles of its southern tip, Tierra del Fuego.

While on this voyage, Vespucci wrote long letters to a friend describing his travels. He was the first to realize that this was a separate continent, not part of Asia. Although he did not captain the ship, his written accounts of what they saw and maps of the areas they explored were what eventually made him famous.

In his letters, Vespucci described the **culture** and people he met in the New World. He included information about the natives' diet, religion, family life, marriage, society, and children. His letters were published in many languages and became very popular.

Amerigo Vespucci was the Italian navigator for whom the continents of North and South America were named.

On his third and final voyage, Vespucci contracted **malaria** and died after he returned to Spain in 1512.

Vespucci did not name the continents of the New World after himself. That was done by a German cartographer, Martin Waldseemuller, who was drawing a new, updated world map. He had read of Vespucci's travels and decided to honor him on his map. He printed and sold his map with the name America on the southern continent of the New World.

Another mapmaker, Gerardus Mercator, was the first to include North and South America on a world map he produced in 1538.

Think About It
If Waldseemuller had decided to name the continent Vespucci, we might now live in the United States of Vespucci!

UNIT ONE: EXPLORATION

Name: _____   Date: _____

Amerigo Vespucci (cont.)

Directions: Complete the following activities.

Matching

_____ 1. cartography

_____ 2. astronomy

_____ 3. navigator

_____ 4. culture

_____ 5. malaria

a. infectious mosquito-borne disease

b. person who plots the ship's course

c. a society's shared values, beliefs, and behaviors

d. art and work of making maps or charts

e. science of the universe, in which the stars, planets, etc., are studied

Fill in the Blanks

1. Like Columbus, Amerigo Vespucci was _____.

2. By observing the conjunction of _____ and the _____, Vespucci was able to calculate how far west he had traveled.

3. Vespucci's second voyage in 1501 was on a _____ ship.

4. _____ _____ _____ is the southern tip of South America.

5. Amerigo Vespucci did not _____ the ship; his written accounts of what they saw and maps of the areas they explored were what eventually made him famous.

Multiple Choice

1. As a young man, which of these was not an interest of Amerigo Vespucci?
   a. cartography
   b. astronomy
   c. mathematics
   d. chemistry

2. What was the role of Amerigo Vespucci aboard ship?
   a. captain
   b. navigator
   c. boatswain
   d. quartermaster

3. What disease did Vespucci contract on his third voyage that led to his death?
   a. malaria
   b. meningitis
   c. typhus
   d. cholera

4. Who was the mapmaker who decided to honor Vespucci by printing and selling a map with the name America on the southern continent of the New World?
   a. Gerardus Mercator
   b. Martin Behaim
   c. Martin Waldseemuller
   d. Juan de lo Cosa

John Cabot

Born: about 1450 in Genoa, Italy
Died: 1499

John Cabot moved to England in 1484, seeking an **opportunity** to explore and obtain the fabulous riches of China. Like Columbus and others of his time, John Cabot thought there must be a sea route to the riches of **Asia** by sailing west instead of east.

After being turned down by **merchants** in Spain and Portugal, Cabot received a **letters patent** from Henry VII of England in 1496. The letters patent gave Cabot the right to discover new lands. Part of the letters patent granted to John Cabot by King Henry VII reads as follows:

Although John Cabot sounds like an English name, he was actually Italian. He lived for a time in Venice and worked as a trader in what we now call the Middle East. In Italy, he was known as Giovanni Caboto.

"Be known that we have given ... to John Cabot, citizen of Venice, and to Lewis, Sebastian and Sancio, sons of the said John ... full and free authority... to sail to all parts, regions and coasts of the eastern, western and northern sea ... to find, discover and investigate whatsoever islands, countries, regions or provinces of heathens and **infidels***, in whatsoever part of the world placed, which before this time were unknown to all Christians."*

Later in 1496, he attempted a voyage, but Cabot and his crew were forced to turn back due to bad weather and lack of food. In May of 1497, Cabot sailed from England on a second voyage, taking a route much further to the north than Columbus had taken. The king provided only one small ship (less than 70 feet

long) called the *Matthew* and a crew of 18. On June 24, they sighted land somewhere in the area known today as Newfoundland. Cabot, like Columbus, was convinced he had found an island off the coast of Asia and called it "new found land."

When he returned to England two months later, he didn't bring any riches, silk, or spices, but he had made a map of part of the North American coast. He also reported that one only had to lower a basket over the side of the boat, and it would be filled with fish. King Henry agreed to finance another voyage. Cabot's ship was joined by four other ships provided by merchants who hoped to cash in on what they thought was a new route to the Orient. They left in May, 1498. One of the merchant ships returned to England for repairs, but the other four, with John Cabot as captain, were never seen again.

UNIT ONE: EXPLORATION

John Cabot (cont.)

Directions: Complete the following activities.

Matching

_____ 1. opportunity

_____ 2. Asia

_____ 3. merchant

_____ 4. letters patent

_____ 5. infidel

a. favorable circumstance with a possible positive outcome

b. government document granting a right or title to something, such as land

c. unbeliever in regards to a particular religion

d. one who buys and sells goods for profit

e. largest of the seven continents; located in the Eastern Hemisphere

Fill in the Blanks

1. John Cabot thought there must be a sea route to the riches of Asia by sailing _____ instead of _____.

2. Cabot received a letters patent from _____ VII of _____ in 1496.

3. In the letters patent, besides John Cabot, his sons, _____, _____, and _____ were listed.

4. On a second voyage, the king provided only one small ship called the _____.

5. After returning on his second voyage, John reported that one only had to lower a basket over the side of the boat, and it would be filled with _____.

Constructed Response

Explain what rights were granted to John Cabot and his sons under the terms of the letters patent.

_____

_____

_____

_____

_____

_____

Sebastian Cabot

After his father, John, was lost at sea in 1499, Sebastian Cabot also sailed in search of an alternate route to the East.

Born: about 1476 in Italy
Died: 1557

Like his father, Sebastian Cabot began his career as a mapmaker. Sebastian claimed he had sailed with his father to North America in 1497, but evidence of that is slim. Many other claims he made during his life have also been questioned by **historians**. Some of his actions have led to the belief that he was not a very honest or **honorable** person.

By convincing King Henry VII of England that he could find a water passageway through North America to the East, Cabot received two ships and support from the king. In 1508, he sailed in search of that shortcut. Sebastian took a northern route like his father had.

Cabot reached the coast of Labrador and sailed north as far as Greenland. Finding ice floes even in the summer convinced Cabot to sail west. There he discovered a waterway that led inland. Cabot followed the waterway (Hudson Strait) to a large body of water (Hudson Bay). Cabot thought he had discovered the passage he had sought.

Cabot's crew, cold and tired of the long voyage, threatened mutiny, so he agreed to return to the main coast and head south, hoping to find another passage in a warmer area. They returned to England after exploring the eastern coast of North America as far south as Cape Hatteras, North Carolina.

While Sebastian Cabot was gone, Henry VII had died, and his son, Henry VIII, refused to finance another voyage. Cabot moved to Spain and appealed to King Charles I, who appointed him as **Pilot Major** (chief navigator) of Spain, but would not agree to finance a voyage. Meanwhile, Cabot secretly continued to try to win support from the king of England.

In 1526, Cabot finally received permission from Charles I for another voyage. His instructions were to follow Magellan's route to the Spice Islands of the East Indies. He sailed with four ships to South America where he heard reports of vast wealth from natives in the area. Cabot abandoned his mission and began an unsuccessful search for gold.

Not having found any great treasures in South America, Cabot returned to Spain in 1530. His officers charged him with abusing his crew and disobeying orders. He was arrested, found guilty, and sentenced to banishment in Africa for three years. King Charles **pardoned** him, and Cabot resumed his position as Pilot Major; however, he continued to maintain contact with the English government, hoping for something better.

In 1547, King Edward VI placed Cabot in charge of England's **maritime** affairs and appointed him Pilot Major of England. He became governor of the Muscovy Company of Merchant Adventurers, an English trading organization dedicated to finding a northern passage to China. Cabot died in 1557, never achieving the wealth he desired nor discovering the sea route to China.

UNIT ONE: EXPLORATION

Name: _____ Date: _____

Sebastian Cabot (cont.)

Directions: Complete the following activities.

Matching

_____ 1. historian
_____ 2. honorable
_____ 3. Pilot Major
_____ 4. pardoned
_____ 5. maritime

a. chief navigator
b. a person who is an authority on history
c. official act of being released from guilt for an offense or crime
d. relating to or pertaining to the sea
e. to deserve honor or respect

Fill in the Blanks

1. Sebastian claimed he had sailed with his father to _____ _____ in 1497.

2. Cabot received two ships and support from the king by convincing King Henry VII that he could find a _____ _____ through North America to the East.

3. In 1526, Charles I's instructions to Cabot were to follow Magellan's route to the _____ Islands of the East Indies.

4. After returning to Spain in 1530, Cabot's officers charged him with _____ his crew and _____ orders.

5. The Muscovy Company of Merchant Adventurers was an English trading organization dedicated to finding a _____ passage to _____.

Critical Thinking

Some historians claim Sebastian Cabot was not an honest or honorable person. From what you've learned, do you agree or disagree? Be sure to give specific details or examples to support your opinion.

_____

_____

_____

_____

_____

_____

Name: _____ Date: _____

Magellan Circumnavigates the Earth

In August of 1519, Ferdinand Magellan sailed from Seville, Spain, with five ships. Although he died before completing the voyage, the *Victoria,* one of his ships, became the first to sail around the world.

Did You Know?
Ferdinand Magellan's parents were members of the Portuguese nobility, but on his voyage, he sailed for Spain.

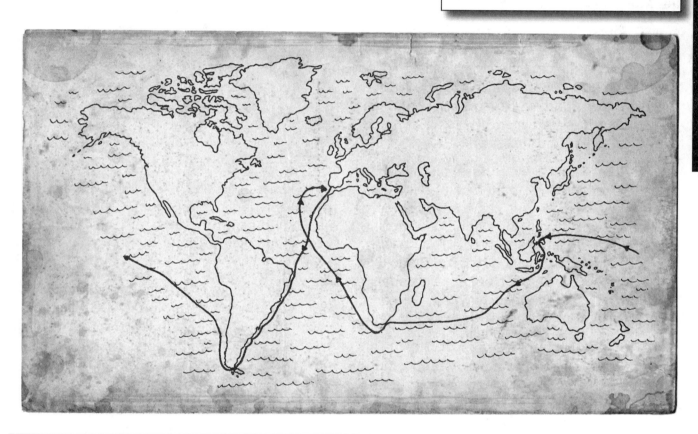

Research
Directions: Use the Internet or other reference sources and the map above to answer the following questions. Write your answers on another sheet of paper.

1. What does *circumnavigate* mean?
2. Why did Ferdinand Magellan make his voyage?
3. Where and how did Magellan die?
4. What continents did Magellan's ships visit on the way?
5. What did Magellan's route prove beyond all doubt?

Juan Ponce de León

Born: about 1460 in León, Spain
Died: 1521

As a boy, Juan Ponce de León was a page in the royal court of Aragon. Later, he served in the army during campaigns against the Muslims in southern Spain.

Ponce de León sailed with Columbus on his second voyage to the New World in 1493. Instead of returning to Spain with Columbus, de León remained in Santo Domingo. He helped the governor subdue a native **insurrection** in 1504. For his services, he was appointed provincial governor of eastern Hispaniola.

Rumors of gold on the island of Borinquen (Puerto Rico) prompted de León to lead a group of settlers to the island in 1509 where they founded the city of Capara (near San Juan). He became the governor of Puerto Rico, but in 1511, King Ferdinand ordered Diego Columbus to replace de León because he was so **ruthless** in his treatment of Native Americans. By then de León was already a wealthy man.

De León heard rumors of Bimini, an island possibly in the Bahamas, where a fountain of youth flowed, surrounded by gold and silver. He received permission to **conquer** and settle Bimini if he could find it. De León sailed from Puerto Rico on March 3, 1513, with three ships. They stopped on several islands, but none held the **mythical** fountain of youth or any great treasures. Finally, on Easter Sunday, de León landed on the coast of Florida near what is now St. Augustine. He called it the land of flowers. At the time, he thought Florida was another island.

De León and his men searched the area for gold, silver, pearls, and the fountain of youth but again found nothing. He sailed south around the Florida Keys and up the west coast

Juan Ponce de León, better known simply as Ponce de León, was the first European to visit Florida.

of Florida near Sanibel Island. They stopped to **replenish** their food and named these islands the Tortugas for the many turtles they found. From there, they returned to Puerto Rico.

The king of Spain knighted de León and appointed him governor of Florida, but first he was commanded to subdue the Carib tribe, which was raiding Puerto Rico. These Native Americans were fierce fighters, able to cross the Caribbean in huge canoes.

In 1521, de León resumed his search for the fountain of youth. He returned to Florida with two ships carrying 200 colonists and many domestic animals. They landed on the west coast of Florida where they were attacked by the Calusa. De León was wounded with a poison arrow. The colonists returned to the ships and sailed back to Cuba where De León died of his wounds.

Ponce de León was buried in San Juan, Puerto Rico. These words were written on his grave: Beneath this stone lie the bones of the valiant Lion (León means lion) whose deeds surpassed the greatness of his name.

Name: _____ Date: _____

Juan Ponce de León (cont.)

Directions: Complete the following activities.

Matching

_____ 1. insurrection   a. cruel; without pity

_____ 2. ruthless   b. imaginary

_____ 3. conquer   c. rebellion or revolt

_____ 4. mythical   d. to fill again

_____ 5. replenish   e. defeat by force

Fill in the Blanks

1. As a boy, Juan Ponce de León was a _____ in the royal court of Aragon.

2. Ponce de León sailed with _____ on his second voyage to the New World in 1493.

3. The king of Spain _____ de León and appointed him _____ of Florida, but first he was commanded to subdue the Carib tribe.

4. De León thought _____ was another island.

5. In 1521, de León resumed his search for the _____ of _____.

Critical Thinking

On de León's tombstone it reads, "Beneath this stone lie the bones of the valiant Lion whose deeds surpassed the greatness of his name." Do you agree with this description of Ponce de León's life? Why or why not? Use specific details or examples to support your decision.

_____

_____

_____

_____

_____

_____

_____

_____

_____

UNIT ONE: EXPLORATION

Hernan Cortés

Born: 1485 in Medellín, Spain
Died: 1547

Hernan Cortés left Spain in 1504 when he was about 19 years old after studying law for a short time at the University of Salamanca. He served as a clerk to Diego Velázquez during the campaign to conquer and settle Cuba.

As the European population of Cuba grew, Velázquez, now governor, realized there wasn't enough land or slave labor on the island. Expeditions sent to the Yucatán Peninsula between 1516 and 1518 found indications of a wealthy civilization. Velázquez decided to send Cortés on an expedition to explore, trade, and search for Christian captives.

Before Cortés left, Velázquez began to suspect that Cortés was not loyal and cancelled his **commission**. Cortés ignored him, recruited soldiers, and sailed to Mexico in 1519.

Cortés founded his own city, Veracruz, in the name of the king of Spain and made himself its leader. Fearing that some of his soldiers might rebel, he burned his fleet so they could not leave.

Cortés then sent word to King Charles I of Spain, asking the king to confirm him as leader of the settlement and seeking permission to lead a "just war" against the ruler of the people of Mexico who had "ungodly ways." He also described the wealth of the Aztecs and his desire to claim it for Christianity and the king. Without waiting for a reply, he set out overland.

With the help of **translators**, Cortés recruited people from other tribes who were hostile to the Aztecs. After a 250-mile march, they arrived at the capital city of Tenochtitlán.

The conquest of the Aztec empire by Hernan Cortés gave Spain a base of power that spread rapidly throughout Central and South America.

The Aztecs believed Cortés fulfilled a **prophesy** that a descendent of a white-skinned, bearded god, Quetzalcóatl, would return from the east to rule the Aztecs. At first, they welcomed the Spaniards with lavish gifts.

Although their meeting started in a friendly manner, relations between the Spaniards and Aztecs soon changed. Perhaps Montezuma, the Aztec emperor, realized that Cortés was not a god. Perhaps Cortés feared they would become human sacrifices or was greedy for more wealth. For whatever reason, Cortés seized Montezuma and held him prisoner. The Aztecs gathered treasures for ransom.

Think About It
Considering they had never seen white-skinned, bearded men, metal armor, or horses, how do you think the Aztecs felt when Cortés and his army arrived?

Hernan Cortés (cont.)

Cortés learned that Velázquez had sent soldiers to return him to Cuba. He captured their leader and persuaded most of the soldiers to join him.

When he returned to Tenochtitlán, Cortés discovered his soldiers had provoked an uprising by killing many Aztecs during a religious ceremony.

Cortés convinced Montezuma to speak to the crowd to try to restore order. Considering him a traitor, the Aztecs threw stones at Montezuma. He was struck in the head and died three days later. A full-scale rebellion began. More than half the Spaniards were killed as they retreated from the city.

Cortés reinforced his army with people from tribes who were enemies of the Aztecs and returned to Tenochtitlán in 1521. They **blockaded** the city, cutting off the supply of food and water. After three months, an outbreak of smallpox further weakened the defenders, and Cortés finally pushed his way into the city. The Spanish army razed the city until hardly any trace of the Aztecs remained. Mexico City was built on the ruins of Tenochtitlán.

Cortés hoped his success would persuade the king to **absolve** him of his rebellion against Velázquez. King Charles I named Cortés governor of New Spain in 1523 and granted him many riches.

Cortés led another expedition to Honduras in 1524. By then, even the king feared Cortés was too ambitious and recalled him to Spain. He gave Cortés the title Marquis of Oaxaca but removed him as governor. When Cortés returned to Mexico, his activities were checked, his property and rights denied, and his popularity declined.

Cortés continued exploring. He discovered the peninsula of Baja California in 1536. When the king granted Francisco Coronado the right to search for the Seven Cities of Cíbola, Cortés returned to Spain to complain. The king ignored Cortés's demands to restore his rights and property. Eventually, Cortés retired to a small estate near Seville, Spain, where he died.

By conquering and destroying a magnificent civilization, Hernan Cortés gave Spain a power base in Mexico that lasted until the nineteenth century. To gain his ends, he killed and enslaved thousands of Native Americans.

UNIT ONE: EXPLORATION

Name: _____ Date: _____

Hernan Cortés (cont.)

Directions: Complete the following activities.

Matching

_____ 1. commission

_____ 2. translator

_____ 3. prophesy

_____ 4. blockaded

_____ 5. absolve

a. to pronounce free from guilt or blame

b. to foretell or predict

c. cut off or isolated

d. authority to perform a task or duty

e. one who interprets or translates from one language to another

Fill in the Blanks

1. Cortés founded his own city, _____, in the name of the king of Spain and made himself its leader.

2. The Aztecs believed Cortés fulfilled a prophesy that a descendant of a white-skinned, bearded god called _____ would return from the east to rule the Aztecs.

3. Cortés seized _____, the Aztec emperor, and held him prisoner.

4. _____ _____ was built on the ruins of the city of Tenochtitlán.

5. Cortés discovered the peninsula of _____ _____ in 1536.

Critical Thinking

Cortés claimed his actions were for the benefit of the king and Christianity. Do you agree or disagree? Give specific details and examples to support your decision.

_____

_____

_____

_____

_____

_____

_____

_____

_____

Francisco Pizarro

Born: about 1475 in Trujillo, Spain
Died: 1541

Francisco Pizarro arrived in Hispaniola in 1502. He joined an expedition to Colombia in 1509. While serving under Vasco de Balboa, he became his chief lieutenant during the march across Panama to the Pacific Ocean. Later, Pizarro became a captain for Pedrarias, the governor of Panama, who had Pizarro arrest Balboa for **treason**.

While in Panama, Pizarro heard rumors of a rich and powerful **empire** located further south. He and a longtime friend, Diego de Almagro, organized an expedition to explore and search for gold in 1524. Two attempts ended in failure. Pizarro returned to Spain and received permission from King Charles I to conquer the Incas and become the governor of Peru. He raised an army and returned to Peru in 1532 with about 180 men.

Pizarro and his soldiers sailed along the coast of South America. The Spaniards found out that the Incas were engaged in a civil war between two brothers, Atahualpa and Huascar, who both wanted to rule the empire. Learning that Atahualpa was in the city of Cajamarca, Pizarro and his troops marched on. Atahualpa sent guides with gifts who helped them along the route. They told Pizarro that Atahualpa had an army of 40,000 warriors.

Pizarro sent Hernando de Soto and 20 men to meet with Atahualpa. De Soto told Atahualpa that Pizarro had 30,000 men in camp and another 10,000 armed men surrounding the city. Pizarro persuaded Atahualpa to attend a huge feast with thousands of his nobles. A priest greeted Atahualpa and gave a long sermon using translators. He told the Incas they must pledge allegiance to the great king and queen of Spain, give up their pagan gods, and

Although he started life in poverty, Francisco Pizarro gained fabulous wealth before he died.

follow Christianity. He handed Atahualpa a Bible, but the Inca chief threw it to the ground. Pizarro's troops, previously hidden, surrounded the Incas, and with the aid of horses and cannon, **slaughtered** most of the guests. They captured Atahualpa and held him for ransom. Atahualpa agreed to fill one large room with gold and two smaller rooms with silver in exchange for his release—over 13,000 pounds of gold and 26,000 pounds of silver. Pizarro accepted the ransom, but then he refused to release Atahualpa. The Spaniards looted the city, torturing and killing thousands. They forced many to become slaves. Fearing Atahualpa would rally the support of the Incas to fight the Spaniards, Pizarro had him executed on August 29, 1533.

The Spaniards marched to the city of Cusco where they defeated the remainder of Atahualpa's followers and looted the city. Pizarro set up the Inca Manco Capac to rule in Cusco as a **puppet leader**, but Pizarro actually ruled from Lima, the new capital of Peru. Pizarro established a system of **forced labor** among the native people.

Conflict occurred between Pizarro and his partner, Diego de Almagro, who claimed Cusco for himself. During the power struggle, Almagro was killed. Almagro's followers took revenge by assassinating Pizarro in his palace in Lima in 1541.

UNIT ONE: EXPLORATION

Name: _____   Date: _____

Francisco Pizarro (cont.)

Directions: Complete the following activities.

Matching

_____ 1. treason

_____ 2. empire

_____ 3. slaughter

_____ 4. puppet leader

_____ 5. forced labor

a. lands ruled by a single authority

b. slavery

c. a leader whose actions and ideas are controlled by another person

d. to kill cruelly; massacre

e. an act of betrayal against your country

Fill in the Blanks

1. Pizarro served as a chief lieutenant under _____ de _____.

2. He and a longtime friend, Diego de Almagro, organized an expedition to explore and search for _____ in 1524.

3. Pizarro captured Atahualpa and held him for _____.

4. Pizarro established a system of forced labor among the _____ people.

5. In 1541, Pizarro was _____ in his palace in Lima by Almagro's followers.

Constructed Response

Describe Francisco Pizarro's relationship with the Incas. Give specific details or examples to support your answer.

_____

_____

_____

_____

_____

_____

_____

_____

UNIT ONE: EXPLORATION

Francisco Vasquez de Coronado

Born: about 1510 in Salamanca, Spain
Died: 1554 in Mexico City

Born to a **noble** family in Spain, Francisco Coronado became friendly with Antonio de Mendoza. When Mendoza was appointed viceroy to New Spain (Mexico) in 1535, Coronado traveled with him. In 1538, Coronado helped put down a rebellion of African slaves.

A year later, Mendoza appointed Coronado as governor of New Galicia, a **province** in western Mexico. From Cabeza de Vaca and Frey Marcos de Niza, they heard stories of natives who wore emeralds and gold in the Seven Golden Cities of Cíbola. Of course, Coronado and Mendoza were very interested.

From the time the first Spaniards ventured to the New World, they had heard stories and legends of fabulous wealth, fountains of youth, and cities of gold. In almost every case, the stories were nothing but rumors or lies. But every once in a while, someone like Hernan Cortés or Francisco Pizarro would discover the truth behind the stories. That was enough **incentive** to lure thousands into leading or joining expeditions in the belief that they would be among the lucky few.

Mendoza, Coronado, and other investors contributed what amounted to several million dollars in today's money to finance the expedition. In 1540, Coronado set off with 340 Spaniards, 300 native allies, and 1,000 Native American and African slaves. They took along herds of cattle, pigs, and sheep.

There was trouble from the beginning. They were slowed down by too many people, too much baggage, and the herds of animals they took for food. A smaller force continued. By

Although he never found the fabled Seven Cities of Cíbola, Francisco Coronado established Spain's claim to a large portion of what later became the southwestern United States.

the time they had traveled 300 miles, Coronado began receiving reports that the stories of the Seven Cities of Cíbola were false. That news must have been a terrible blow to Coronado, who had invested much of his wife's money and his reputation in the expedition.

Part of Coronado's expedition continued to march north into Arizona and then northeast to New Mexico, hungry, thirsty, and suffering as they crossed the deserts. There they found the first of the seven cities, but it was not a fabulous city of gold. What they found were the simple pueblos of the Zuni and natives willing to fight to defend their homes. Coronado conquered the Zuni there and in other areas, but nowhere did he find any great cities of gold.

Over the winter, Coronado heard stories from an Indian slave of Quivira, a rich city to the northeast. With 30 men, Coronado followed his guide to central Kansas where they found the Wichita people living in tepees. When the slave confessed he had invented the story, Coronado had him executed, and he returned to his base in New Mexico.

UNIT ONE: EXPLORATION

Francisco Vasquez de Coronado (cont.)

In the meantime, Coronado had sent various groups off to explore the area. One group, led by Garcia López de Cárdenas, discovered the spectacular Grand Canyon. Another group found the **fertile** Rio Grande valley. Melchor Díaz discovered that lower California was a peninsula, not an island. Upon reaching the banks of the Colorado River, he became the first European to travel by land from Mexico to California.

During his journey to Kansas, Coronado and his group were the first Europeans to see and describe the great herds of American bison. They explored along the Kansas and Arkansas Rivers. In all, they had traveled nearly 3,000 miles from Mexico to a point approximately in the center of what is today the United States. All of this land they claimed for Spain.

Coronado was badly injured in a fall from a horse. A fortuneteller in Spain had predicted he would become rich, famous, and powerful but would eventually fall from a horse and never recover. Although some of his officers wanted to continue to explore, Coronado decided to return to Mexico. Only about 100 of his men returned with him.

Coronado remained governor until 1544, when he was charged with **corruption**, **negligence**, and cruelty to the Native Americans. He retired to Mexico City where he died in 1554.

Map Activity

Coronado and his expeditions traveled though what later became California, New Mexico, Arizona, Texas, Oklahoma, Arkansas, and Kansas. Label these states on the map.

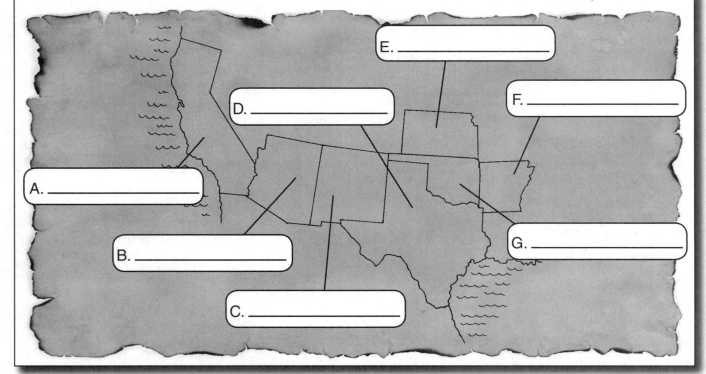

E. _____

D. _____

F. _____

A. _____

B. _____

G. _____

C. _____

Hernando de Soto

Born: about 1500 in Barcarrota, Spain
Died: 1542

After spending several years as an **aide** to the governor of Panama, Hernando de Soto joined Francisco Pizarro in 1530 on the coast of Ecuador and became his second-in-command.

Pizarro led the Spanish army south to Caxamarca, Peru. He and de Soto **lured** the Inca emperor into a trap and held him **hostage** until they received millions of dollars in gold in ransom. Then Pizarro executed the emperor.

De Soto returned to Spain in 1536, rich and famous, but he wanted more. He wanted power. After marrying the daughter of the governor of Panama, de Soto asked King Charles I of Spain to **appoint** him as governor of Colombia and Ecuador. The king feared Pizarro and de Soto would join together and set up a powerful empire of their own in South America. Instead, King Charles appointed de Soto governor of Cuba and Florida and gave him the authority to explore and conquer Florida for Spain. Like others, de Soto had heard rumors of cities of gold and a fountain of youth hidden in Florida.

In 1538, de Soto sailed from Spain with his wife and a large army. Upon arrival in Havana, Cuba, de Soto set his wife up as governor. With 1,000 soldiers, de Soto sailed to Tampa Bay, Florida. In Tampa Bay, they found a Spaniard, Juan Ortiz, living with Native Americans. Ortiz had come to Florida 10 years earlier, been captured, and had lived with them since. Ortiz became their guide and helped them make peace with the natives.

However, that peace did not last. De Soto and his army marched off to conquer the natives and search for gold and the fountain

Like thousands of other Spanish soldiers, Hernando de Soto came to the New World in search of gold.

of youth. De Soto made enemies by stealing crops, burning villages, and **enslaving** the people.

While searching for gold, de Soto and his soldiers explored much of what later became the southeastern United States, including parts of Florida, North and South Carolina, Tennessee, Georgia, Alabama, Mississippi, Arkansas, and Texas.

Along the way, many men died of sickness, in attacks, and from insect and snake bites. After a battle at Movilla, a large Choctaw city, de Soto lost many more men. Most of their equipment and horses were gone too. His men urged him to return home, but de Soto refused to give up his dreams of wealth and power.

In 1541, de Soto and his group became the first Europeans to see the Mississippi River. In the spring of 1542, de Soto fell ill and died. His aide buried him in the river to keep his death a secret from the natives.

Name: _____   Date: _____

Hernando de Soto (cont.)

Directions: Complete the following activities.

Matching

_____ 1. aide

_____ 2. lure

_____ 3. hostage

_____ 4. appoint

_____ 5. enslaving

a. to entice with the promise of reward or pleasure

b. to select or designate

c. the act of making someone a slave

d. someone forcibly detained until the captor's demands are met

e. assistant

Fill in the Blanks

1. Hernando de Soto joined _____ _____ in 1530 on the coast of Ecuador and became his second-in-command.

2. The king feared Pizarro and de Soto would join together and set up a powerful empire of their own in _____ _____.

3. De Soto made enemies by _____ crops, burning _____, and enslaving the people.

4. In 1541, de Soto and his group became the first _____ to see the Mississippi River.

5. De Soto was buried in the _____ to keep his death a secret from the _____.

Graphic Organizer

Describe de Soto's interaction with each person or group in the boxes below.

Francisco Pizarro

Native Americans

Hernando de Soto

His Men

King Charles I

Jacques Cartier

Born: 1491 in Saint Malo, France
Died: 1557

Not much is known of the early life of Jacques Cartier. He grew up in a **seaport** on the northwestern coast of France. In 1534, King Francis I of France allowed Cartier to lead an **expedition** to search for a water passage across North America to the Pacific Ocean.

On his first voyage, Cartier crossed the Atlantic Ocean with two ships and 60 men in only 20 days, about half the time the voyage usually took. He landed first on an **island** near Newfoundland, then sailed north and west, exploring several inland waterways including the Strait of Belle Isle and the Gulf of St. Lawrence. Landing near the site of Gaspe, Cartier claimed the land for France. Since it was late autumn by then, Cartier decided to return to France.

Although he had not found the passage he sought, Cartier told the king of France he had heard of another large river that he hoped would lead to the Pacific Ocean. The king authorized a second voyage in 1535, this time with three ships.

Cartier reached the St. Lawrence River and sailed upriver to the present location of Quebec. There he found Stadacona, a Huron village. The chief, Donnaconna, welcomed the men to *canada,* the Huron word for village. The expedition continued on to Hochelaga, a **fortified** village of the Ottawas near where the city of Montreal was later built. Cartier learned that if he continued, he would soon encounter rapids too dangerous for his ships to navigate. Disappointed, he sailed back to Stadacona where they stayed for the winter. Cartier heard stories from the Hurons about a land in the north called Saguenay, filled with gold and other treasures.

While the Spanish explored South America and the southern United States, France commissioned Jacques Cartier to search for a waterway west to the Pacific Ocean.

When he returned to France, Cartier had to admit that he still had not found the promised **passageway**, that many of his men had died, and that he had brought no riches back for the king.

In 1541, the king gave Cartier permission for a third voyage, but not as the leader. This time he would be the assistant to Jean-Francois de la Rocque, sieur de Roberval, Viceroy to New France. Cartier set sail on his third voyage in 1541 without Roberval. Cartier returned to the Huron village of Stadacona. While waiting for Roberval to arrive, he traded for beaver pelts and other furs. Then he continued his quest for the riches of Saguenay.

In the spring, Cartier returned to Newfoundland to discover Roberval had finally arrived—a year late. Roberval wanted Cartier to go back to Stadacona, but Cartier refused and returned to France. He married and settled down on a small country estate close to Saint Malo. He died on September 1, 1557.

Name: _____   Date: _____

Jacques Cartier (cont.)

Directions: Complete the following activities.

Matching

_____ 1. seaport

_____ 2. expedition

_____ 3. island

_____ 4. fortified

_____ 5. passageway

a. town or harbor that can be accessed by seagoing vessels

b. body of land completely surrounded by water

c. has been secured or made strong

d. journey

e. connecting corridor

Fill in the Blanks

1. In 1534, King Francis I of France allowed Cartier to lead an expedition to search for a water passage across _____ America to the _____ Ocean.

2. On his first voyage, Cartier crossed the _____ Ocean with two ships and 60 men in only 20 days.

3. The Huron chief, Donnaconna, welcomed the men to _____ , the Huron word for village.

4. Cartier heard stories from the Hurons about a land in the north called _____, filled with gold and other treasures.

5. In 1541, the king gave Cartier permission for a third voyage, but not as the _____.

Graphic Organizer

Complete the following chart based upon the voyages of Jacques Cartier.

Cartier's Accomplishments	Cartier's Failures

Samuel de Champlain

Born: 1567 in Brouage, France
Died: 1635 in Quebec, Canada

Little is known of Samuel de Champlain's early life. From his father, a sea captain, he learned navigation and mapmaking. Champlain served in the army of France's King Henry IV for several years. His first known voyage was a two-year trip with his uncle around 1599 to Puerto Rico, Mexico, Colombia, the Bermudas, and Panama.

Champlain presented the king with detailed reports and drawings of what he had seen in Central and South America. He was invited by Aymar de Chaste, a fur trader, to join an expedition to Canada in 1603.

When Champlain arrived, he found the Algonquins and Hurons were in the midst of a war with their enemies, the Iroquois. Champlain and other Frenchmen became allies of the Algonquins and Hurons to protect the French fur trading interests. This **alliance** later caused many problems for French and English colonists.

From the natives, Champlain learned of a "great water" to the west. Champlain hoped this would be the Pacific Ocean. At last he might be the one who found the **elusive** water route to India!

Champlain returned to the king of France with his news. The following year he sailed again to Canada as mapmaker and **geographer** with a group planning to establish a colony. They explored the North American coast as far south as present-day Cape Cod, Massachusetts.

After building a fort at Port Royal, Champlain explored the area and established friendly **relations** with the Micmacs and other natives before returning to France.

By 1608, Champlain was back in Canada. He chose Stadacona as the most suitable place for a new colony. This eventually became Quebec and was the first **permanent** city in North America north of Florida to be settled by Europeans.

Samuel de Champlain wrote to a friend in 1613 that he had acquired an interest "from a very young age in the art of navigation, along with a love of the high seas."

Champlain made several trips between France and Canada. In France, he pleaded with the king for supplies, finances, and people for the colonies. In Canada, he continued to explore lands and waterways to the west and south. He named one of the lakes he discovered for himself, Lake Champlain. He helped establish another colony that later became Montreal. Champlain also became further involved in the war of the Hurons and Algonquins against the Iroquois, and he was wounded several times.

France and England went to war in 1628. The following year, Quebec was captured by the British. Champlain was taken to England as a prisoner. By then, however, the war had ended. Champlain returned to Canada in 1633 as governor of New France to find Quebec in ruins. He worked to rebuild the city, expand the fur trade, and encourage colonists until his death in 1635.

Name: _____   Date: _____

Samuel de Champlain (cont.)

Directions: Complete the following activities.

Matching

_____ 1. alliance

_____ 2. elusive

_____ 3. geographer

_____ 4. relations

_____ 5. permanent

a. opposite of temporary

b. association or connection

c. someone who studies the earth's geography

d. to join together for a common goal

e. to evade

Fill in the Blanks

1. From his father, a sea captain, Champlain learned _____ and _____

2. Champlain and other Frenchmen became allies of the Algonquins and Hurons to protect the French _____ _____ interests.

3. Stadacona eventually became _____.

4. He named one of the lakes he discovered for himself, _____ _____.

5. Champlain returned to Canada in 1633 as _____ of New France to find Quebec in ruins.

Critical Thinking

Champlain has been called the "Father of New France." Do you think he deserves this title? Why or why not? Support your opinion with specific details or examples.

_____

_____

_____

_____

_____

_____

_____

_____

_____

_____

UNIT ONE: EXPLORATION

Henry Hudson

Born: about 1570 in England
Died: date unknown, possibly 1611

Henry Hudson was commissioned by the English Muscovy Company in 1607 to find a shortcut from England to "the islands of spicery." Some geographers **theorized** that since the days were longer the further north you went, once you got to the Arctic, the sun would be warm enough to melt the ice, and you would eventually reach open water.

As they sailed north, the magnetic needle of the compass was affected, leading crewmen to believe it was caused by an evil spell. They threatened to **mutiny**.

Hudson sailed to Greenland and north, searching for a passage through the Arctic Ocean to the Far East. Hudson failed in his first two attempts when he ran into **ice floes**, but he did sail farther north than any other previous explorer—about 577 nautical miles from the North Pole.

On his second voyage for the Muscovy Company in 1608, Hudson sailed through the Arctic waters north of Russia as far as Novaya Zemlya. Again, ice blocked the ship, and he had to return to England.

The Dutch East India Company of the Netherlands, which had a **monopoly** on trade with the Orient, also wanted to shorten the lengthy and expensive route around the southern tip of Africa. They hired Hudson in 1609, provided a ship, the *Halve Maan (Half Moon),* and a crew of Dutch and English sailors. Again Hudson tried sailing east, north of Norway, but soon turned his ship around and headed for the New World.

Hudson sailed to North America and explored the river later named for him, going as

Little is known of Henry Hudson's early life. He probably had experience sailing because by the time of his first recorded voyage, he was already a captain.

far as present-day Albany, New York, before the river became too shallow to continue. Because Hudson had been sent by a company from the Netherlands, the Dutch later laid claim to land in this area. When he returned to England, he was arrested for sailing under another nation's flag. The *Half Moon* and its Dutch crew went home. Hudson was commanded to serve only England.

The following year, a group of wealthy London merchants sent Hudson on another voyage as captain of the *Discovery,* still in search of a northwest passage. Hudson sailed to Iceland, into the Hudson Strait, and on to Hudson Bay. Trapped by ice in James Bay, the crew was forced to winter there. Over the winter, the crew mutinied and set Hudson, his son, and seven others **adrift** in a small open boat in 1611. They were never seen again. Three years later, at the insistence of his wife, Katherine, the Dutch East India Company sent a ship to look for Hudson and his men, but no trace of them was ever found.

UNIT ONE: EXPLORATION

Name: _____ Date: _____

Henry Hudson (cont.)

Directions: Complete the following activities.

Matching

_____ 1. theorized

_____ 2. mutiny

_____ 3. ice floe

_____ 4. monopoly

_____ 5. adrift

   a. to rebel against lawful authority

   b. to have formed a theory

   c. complete control over a product or service

   d. to float without being anchored

   e. a single piece, large or small, of floating sea ice

Fill in the Blanks

1. Henry Hudson was commissioned by the English Muscovy Company in 1607 to find a shortcut from _____ to "the islands of spicery."

2. Hudson sailed to Greenland and north, searching for a passage through the Arctic Ocean to the _____ _____.

3. On his second voyage for the Muscovy Company in 1608, Hudson sailed through the Arctic waters north of _____ as far as Novaya Zemlya.

4. Because Hudson had been sent by a company from the Netherlands when he explored the area of North America that would become New York, the _____ later laid claim to land in this area.

5. Over the winter, the crew _____ and set Hudson, his son, and seven others adrift in a small open boat in 1611.

Critical Thinking

Even before Columbus, it was common for captains from one country to sail for a foreign monarch. Why do you think England arrested Henry Hudson and commanded him to serve only England?

_____

_____

_____

_____

_____

_____

_____

René Robert Cavelier, sieur de La Salle

Born: November 22, 1643, in Rouen, France
Died: 1687

Historical sources agree that Robert La Salle spent eight or nine years studying with the **Jesuits**, but they do not agree on whether or not he became a priest. He immigrated to Canada in 1666 and was **granted** land on the St. Lawrence River, where he became a trader. From 1669 to 1670, he explored the region south of Lakes Ontario and Erie, discovering the Ohio River in 1671.

During his travels, La Salle became familiar with many of the Native American tribes, their languages, and customs. He was appointed commander of Fort Frontenac (Kingston, Ontario), a trading station, and put in charge of the fur trade in that area.

La Salle heard tales of a great river system that he thought might flow across North America. Like others before him, he hoped to find a water passage across the continent. He began his first major explorations in 1669.

In 1677, La Salle received permission to explore and trade to the west. He established forts at the mouth of the St. Joseph River and along the Illinois River.

La Salle and a party of French and Native Americans sailed down the Mississippi River to the Gulf of Mexico in 1682. He claimed all land drained by the river for Louis XIV, king of France, and named the region Louisiana.

When La Salle returned to France in 1683, the king received him as a hero and named him **Viceroy** of North America. The following year, he sent La Salle with four ships to establish a colony for France at the mouth of the Mississippi River. They sailed

The French explorer Robert La Salle explored the length of the Mississippi River, claiming the entire area for France.

around Florida, through the Gulf of Mexico, and landed on the shore of Matagorda Bay, Texas. At first, La Salle believed the bay was the western outlet of the Mississippi River but then realized his mistake. Of his four ships, two sank, one was captured by the Spanish, and the other returned to France, leaving the colonists stranded and without supplies. Many died from disease, rattlesnake bites, and attacks by unfriendly natives.

La Salle and a small group of men set out for Canada in 1687 on foot, leaving behind about 20 settlers. His men mutinied and killed him near the Trinity River in Texas. A few of the survivors eventually made it to Quebec.

The *Belle,* one of La Salle's supply ships that sank in 1686, was discovered in Matagorda Bay in 1995 in only 12 feet of water. Marine archaeologists have recovered the hull of the ship and one skeleton. There were also bronze cannons bearing the **crest** of Louis XIV; thousands of blue, white, and black glass trade beads; and other **artifacts** well preserved in the sand and mud.

Name: _____   Date: _____

René Robert Cavelier, sieur de La Salle (cont.)

Directions: Complete the following activities.

Matching

_____ 1. Jesuits

_____ 2. granted

_____ 3. Viceroy

_____ 4. crest

_____ 5. artifacts

a. physical objects that are of historical or archaeological interest

b. given legal rights or privileges

c. coat of arms

d. person ruling a country, province, or colony as the representative of the king or queen

e. members of a Roman Catholic religious order founded by St. Ignatius Loyola dedicated to missionary and educational work

Fill in the Blanks

1. La Salle explored the region south of Lakes Ontario and Erie, discovering the _____ River in 1671.

2. La Salle established _____ at the mouth of the St. Joseph River and along the Illinois River.

3. La Salle claimed all land drained by the Mississippi River for Louis XIV, king of France, and named the region _____.

4. The king sent La Salle with four ships to establish a colony for _____ at the mouth of the Mississippi River.

5. La Salle's men _____ and killed him near the Trinity River.

Graphic Organizer

Complete the chart below based on the explorations of René Robert Cavelier, sieur de La Salle.

PURPOSES OF EXPLORATION	OBSTACLES HE HAD TO OVERCOME	HIS ACCOMPLISHMENTS

Searching for the Explorers

Directions: Match the first and last names of these famous explorers.

_____ 1. Amerigo
_____ 2. Christopher
_____ 3. Francisco
_____ 4. Francisco Vasquez
_____ 5. Henry
_____ 6. Hernan
_____ 7. Hernando
_____ 8. Jacques
_____ 9. Ferdinand
_____ 10. John
_____ 11. Leif
_____ 12. Ponce
_____ 13. Robert
_____ 14. Samuel
_____ 15. Vasco

A. Balboa
B. Cabot
C. Cartier
D. Champlain
E. Columbus
F. Coronado
G. Cortés
H. de León
I. de Soto
J. Erikson
K. Hudson
L. La Salle
M. Magellan
N. Pizarro
O. Vespucci

Directions: Look up, down, backward, forward, and diagonally to find the first and last names (separately) of the explorers in the puzzle.

```
D M A G E L L A N O Q D N R O C S A V N C B C J L
N R Q G K N N C R B T F Z B M M R K G M R L W Z H
T C Q X B O P E N F L O N J R P W Q P M W C X N G
Q C W M S H I C B D R N S E Y C N S Q I O M G O N
K R L D E T H L L C W A H E N V C Z E R Z N R S L
B G U R R C V R W O P N K D A L N T U T A P K N
Q H N A J P R R N G O L Z C K Y O E W Y Q Z R I Y
J A C H B L O W J T Q F U K I B S B Q K Q C H R K
N H L E R B B N S T H N P M M S Y K L M F W A E O
T D W N P K E I C H B F M C B Y C X G A Q M B J Q
D N L R K T R M Z E T M Q Y K U M O B D B Z K R T
M A M Y M H T R J T J L E I F F S N H Y K H V B K
W N H W C C N V D F R A N C I S C O V A S Q U E Z
V I O K V O M E M J K L G D Q N K H N L V C W B D
P D G Q H R R S D K C N F V H S T X N O E L E D Q
L R I L W O T P R M M M Z O A F W W Q R K R D T
X E R C D N O U R P G X J M W C H A M P L A I N T
R F E P T A B C C P G M U F T M G O D N A N R E H
W L M D T D A C B J N E R D H L A S A L L E M L X
M N A K W O C I X V L K L L R T T T Y P B K R H B
```

Name: _____ Date: _____

Where Were the Explorers Born?

Directions: Write the last names of these explorers on the lines by the country where they were born. Review what you learned or use reference sources to help you.

1. Vasco Núñez de Balboa
2. John Cabot
3. Sebastian Cabot
4. Jacques Cartier
5. Samuel de Champlain
6. Christopher Columbus
7. Francisco Vasquez de Coronado
8. Hernan Cortés

9. Hernando de Soto
10. Vasco da Gama
11. Henry Hudson
12. Robert La Salle
13. Juan Ponce de León
14. Ferdinand Magellan
15. Francisco Pizarro
16. Amerigo Vespucci

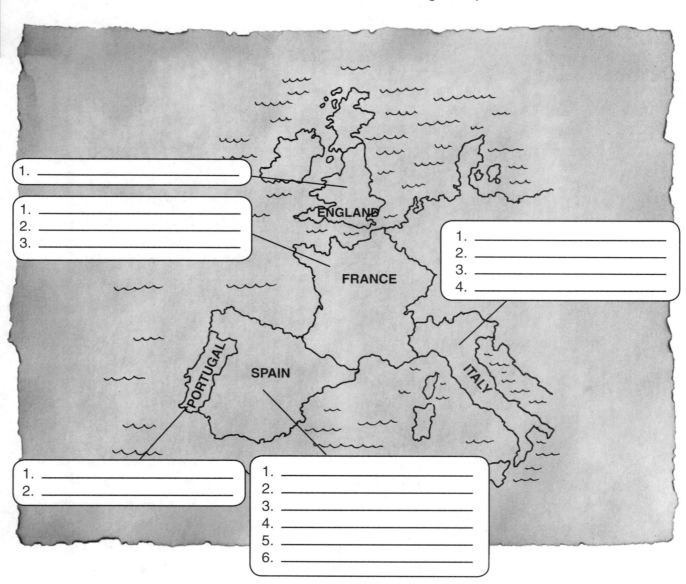

Name: _____   Date: _____

Comparing Explorers

Research

Directions: Learn more about the lives of two of the explorers listed below. Using the information, complete the Venn diagram. Include ways the explorers were alike in the center of the two circles and ways they were different in the two outer parts of the circles.

1. Vasco Núñez de Balboa
2. John Cabot
3. Sebastian Cabot
4. Jacques Cartier
5. Samuel de Champlain
6. Christopher Columbus
7. Francisco Vasquez de Coronado
8. Hernan Cortés

9. Hernando de Soto
10. Vasco da Gama
11. Henry Hudson
12. Robert de La Salle
13. Juan Ponce de León
14. Ferdinand Magellan
15. Francisco Pizarro
16. Amerigo Vespucci

UNIT ONE: EXPLORATION

Name #1: _____   Name #2: _____

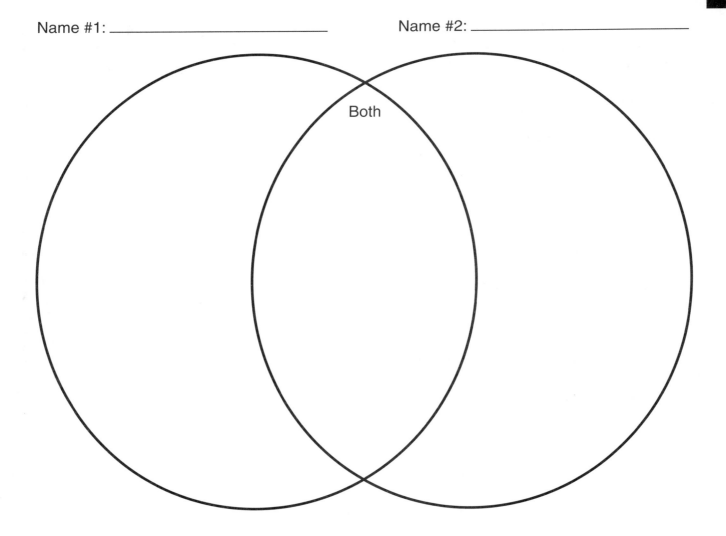

Both

Name: _____   Date: _____

Interview an Explorer

Directions: You are a journalist with a once-in-a-lifetime opportunity to interview Hernan Cortés, Francisco Pizarro, Ponce de León, or Francisco Vasquez de Coronado for your newspaper. Which of these explorers would you interview? Explain your reasons for selecting this explorer.

_____

_____

_____

_____

_____

_____

Research

Directions: After selecting an explorer, research the explorer's life. Using your research, on a separate sheet of paper, answer the following interview questions from the explorer's point of view. (Example: Who were your parents? Answer: My parents were Henry and Mary Jones.)

1. Where were you born?

2. What is your date of birth?

3. On how many voyages did you go?

4. What country sponsored each of your voyages?

5. Where did you explore?

6. What was your purpose for exploration?

7. What problems or obstacles did you have to overcome?

8. What were the major accomplishments of your life?

9. When and where did you die?

10. What was the cause of your death?

11. How old were you at the time of your death?

Time Line of Colonial America

1565	St. Augustine, Florida, founded by Pedro Menendez
1584	Sir Walter Raleigh landed on Roanoke Island
1607	Jamestown, Virginia, colony founded
1613	Dutch trading post established on Manhattan
1619	First Africans brought to the Americas as indentured servants
1620	Pilgrims landed and formed Plymouth colony
1624	Dutch colonists arrived in New Netherlands
1626	Peter Minuit bought the island of Manhattan and named it New Amsterdam
1630	Boston, Massachusetts, founded by John Winthrop
1633	First public school opened in America
1634	Catholic colony founded in Maryland
1636	Providence, Rhode Island, founded by Roger Williams
1636	Harvard College founded in Boston
1638	Anne Hutchinson banished from Massachusetts for religious reasons
1638	First Swedish settlers arrived at Fort Christina, Delaware
1640	First book printed in America: *The Whole Booke of Psalmes*
1652	Rhode Island declared slavery illegal
1673	Jacques Marquette and Louis Joliet explore the Mississippi River
1682	Robert La Salle claimed area along the Mississippi River for France; named it Louisiana
1683	Quaker colony founded in Pennsylvania by William Penn
1692	Witchcraft trials in Salem, Massachusetts
1700	Boston (population 7,000) became largest colonial city
1718	New Orleans founded by the French
1731	First public library opened in Philadelphia
1732	Benjamin Franklin published first *Poor Richard's Almanack*
1733	England passed the Molasses Act, taxing molasses, rum, and sugar
1754	French and Indian War began
1760	Bray School for African-American children opened in Williamsburg
1763	Treaty of Paris ended French and Indian War
1764	England imposed Sugar Act, taxing colonists on lumber, molasses, rum, and other foods
1767	England passed Townshend Acts, taxing colonists on glass, paper, and tea
1770	Boston Massacre
1770	Townshend Acts repealed, except tax on tea
1773	Boston Tea Party
1774	First Continental Congress met in Philadelphia
1775	Revolutionary War began
1776	Declaration of Independence adopted by Constitutional Congress
1783	Peace treaty signed with England ended the Revolutionary War

UNIT TWO: THE COLONIES

Name: _____ Date: _____

Colonial America Time Line Activity

Directions: Use the information from the time line of colonial America to answer the questions below.

Short Answer

1. What year was the Declaration of Independence adopted by the Constitutional Congress?

    _____

2. In 1770, the Townshend Acts were repealed except for the tax on what item? _____

3. Who published *Poor Richard's Almanack* in 1732? _____

4. When did the first public school open in America? _____

5. In what year was New Orleans founded by the French? _____

6. What war began in 1754? _____

7. What year did the Revolutionary War begin? _____

8. What was the title of the first book printed in America in 1640? _____

    _____

9. What did Rhode Island declare to be illegal in 1652? _____

10. What year was the Jamestown colony founded in Virginia? _____

Multiple Choice

11. What year did the Boston Tea Party happen?
    a. 1565   b. 1630   c. 1773   d. 1776

12. What year did the first public library open in Philadelphia?
    a. 1634   b. 1636   c. 1731   d. 1732

13. What year did the Treaty of Paris end the French and Indian War?
    a. 1683   b. 1718   c. 1733   d. 1763

14. What year did the Dutch colonists arrive in New Netherlands?
    a. 1584   b. 1624   c. 1673   d. 1700

15. What year was Harvard College founded in Boston?
    a. 1636   b. 1652   c. 1692   d. 1718

Name: _____   Date: _____

Colonizing the New World

New Spain: Spain was the first European nation to send colonists to the New World. The first Spanish colonies were in Cuba, Puerto Rico, Mexico, and South America. Explorers searched for gold and silver, items that helped make Spain a major power in Europe for over 100 years. St. Augustine, Florida, settled in 1565, was the first permanent European colony in North America.

New France: Although the French were the first to explore the northern part of North America extensively, they were more interested in the fishing banks off the coast of Newfoundland and furs obtained by trade with the Native Americans. The first permanent French colony in North America was Quebec, founded by Samuel de Champlain in 1608 as a trading post.

New England: Although England was rather a latecomer to colonization, that country sent more people (about 400,000) and established more permanent agricultural communities than any other European nation during the seventeenth century. Few English explorers or adventurers had visited North or South America prior to the settlement of Jamestown in 1607. The two major reasons for migrating from England to the New World were religious freedom and acquisition of land.

New Netherlands: Although the Dutch established a string of strong agricultural settlements in the New York area, those settlements were eventually taken over by the English.

New Sweden: The first Swedish colony was founded at Fort Christina, Delaware, in 1638. That and other Swedish colonies were taken over by the Dutch in 1655 and finally by England in 1664.

Activity

Directions: Pretend your classroom is a colony. On a separate sheet of paper, design a flag or banner to represent this colony. Consider the importance of symbolism and choice of color to a flag design.

Name: _____ Date: _____

Why Did People Become Colonists?

People left their homes to travel to a new, unknown land for many reasons. Some sought adventure and riches. Some left because they were not allowed to practice their religions. Others did not like the way the government was run. Some were poor and wanted a chance to own land and have a better life. They were looking for a brighter future for themselves and their families.

People from every social class, religion, and occupation immigrated to the colonies. Doctors, merchants, business people, and lawyers became colonists. So did craftsmen, fur trappers, soldiers, and farmers. They came alone or with friends and families.

Most of the early colonists were from Europe, mainly England, France, Scotland, Sweden, Spain, Germany, Ireland, and the Netherlands. No matter what country they were from, what their occupation had been, or where in the colonies they settled, the first priority of colonists was to survive. To do that, they needed food and shelter.

Graphic Organizer

Directions: Working in a group, create a list of ten things that colonists would have had to do within a short time after arriving in America. After your group completes its list, each group will share their list with the class. Compile the results to determine what the class selects as its top ten. Use the Venn diagram to compare your group's list to the class's list.

Group's List	On Both Lists	Class Top Ten

Name: _____   Date: _____

The Original Thirteen Colonies

Directions: Use a historical atlas to locate the original thirteen colonies. Match the letter on the map to the name of the colony at the right. Then on the map, color the New England colonies red, the Middle Colonies blue, and the Southern Colonies green.

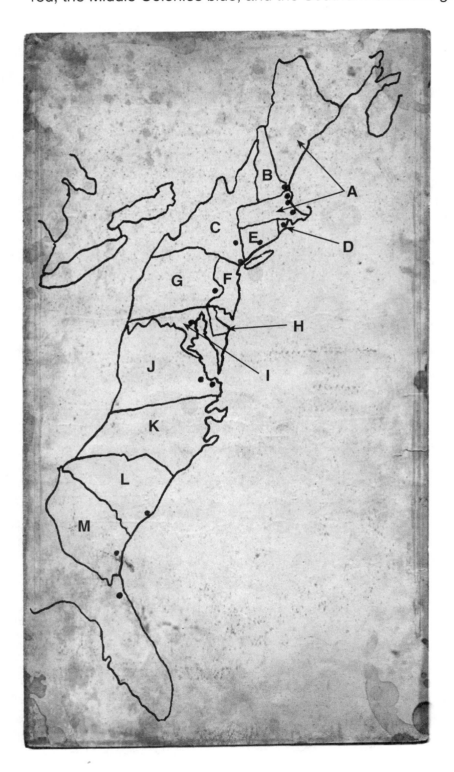

_____ 1. Connecticut

_____ 2. Delaware

_____ 3. Georgia

_____ 4. Maryland

_____ 5. Massachusetts

_____ 6. New Hampshire

_____ 7. New Jersey

_____ 8. New York

_____ 9. North Carolina

_____ 10. Pennsylvania

_____ 11. Rhode Island

_____ 12. South Carolina

_____ 13. Virginia

UNIT TWO: THE COLONIES

Name: _____ Date: _____

The Kitchen—The Heart of the Colonial Home

Colonists spent much of the time in their kitchens. The large fireplace used for cooking and baking made the kitchen the warmest room in the house. The fireplace also provided a source of light. Even when they had houses with several rooms, people often slept in the kitchen in cold weather, gathered there with friends, did their homework, read, sewed, and played games there.

If you could travel back in time to a colonial kitchen, the first thing you would notice is how different it is from a modern-day kitchen. For example, since a system for delivering and using electricity hadn't been invented yet, you would not see a microwave. There are some items, however, like salt, that you would find in both kitchens.

Directions: In the blank beside each word, place a (**C**) if the item would be found only in a colonial kitchen, an (**M**) if it would be found only in a modern-day kitchen, or a (**B**) if it could be found in both a colonial and a modern-day kitchen.

_____ 1. paper towels

_____ 2. waffle iron

_____ 3. sugar cutter

_____ 4. quern

_____ 5. spoon

_____ 6. wooden trencher

_____ 7. electric stove

_____ 8. piggin

_____ 9. refrigerator

_____ 10. tea

_____ 11. bread toaster

_____ 12. flour

_____ 13. can opener

_____ 14. samp mortar

_____ 15. plastic bowl

Think About It

In 1787, a book titled *A Pretty Little Pocket Book* was published. One of the chapters is called "Behaviour at the Table." Here are some of the rules:

Come not to the Table without having your Hands and Face washed, and your Head combed.

Sit not down until thou art bidden by thy parents or other Superiours.

Find no Fault with any Thing that is given thee.

Lean not thy Elbow on the Table, or on the Back of thy Chair.

Name: _____ Date: _____

Baking Bread

Baking bread was a job usually done once a week by colonial women. To bake enough bread for a family took a lot of time and work. Loaves of homemade bread were also given as gifts to friends or neighbors.

To bake bread, women mixed the ingredients in large bowls. It takes about four cups of flour for one loaf of bread. Imagine the size of the bowl needed to mix the ingredients for 10 loaves of bread! The ingredients needed for baking bread depended on the recipe used. Flour, water, salt, and yeast were the main ingredients.

After mixing the ingredients with a wooden spoon, they formed the dough into a ball and let it "rest" for a few minutes. Then they kneaded the dough. Kneading dough was hard work. It involved pressing, stretching, and pounding the dough and then forming it into a ball.

After kneading the dough, they covered it and let it rise in a warm place until it doubled in size (1–2 hours). Then they punched it down, formed it into loaves, and placed the dough in pans to rise again (1–2 hours).

Finally, the bread was ready to bake. Of course, that meant the baker had to gather wood and start a fire in the baking oven so it would be hot enough at the right time. Another 30 to 45 minutes in the oven, and the family would have fresh bread for dinner.

One no-knead bread that was very popular in the southern colonies was Sally Lunn Bread. There are several versions of the story concerning the origin of this bread. One version is that in 1680, Sally Lunn, a Huguenot refugee, immigrated from France to Bath, England. She went to work in a bakery and baked a rich, sweet bread. It was very popular and became known as Sally Lunn Bread.

Today, many people use bread machines to bake fresh bread. The process is much simpler. Pour water, bread mix, and yeast into the pan. Plug in the machine, and set the timer. Wait about three hours, and the bread is ready.

UNIT TWO: THE COLONIES

Activity

Directions: Use the recipe below to make Sally Lunn Bread.

Sally Lunn Bread Recipe

1 cup milk	$\frac{1}{3}$ cup sugar	$\frac{1}{4}$ cup water
$\frac{1}{2}$ cup butter	2 teaspoons salt	3 eggs
4 cups all-purpose flour	2 pkgs. active dry yeast	

Grease a 10-inch tube cake pan. Heat the milk, butter and $\frac{1}{4}$ cup water to about 120°F. Combine together $1\frac{1}{3}$ cups of the flour, sugar, salt, and yeast in a large mixing bowl. Blend the milk mixture into the flour mixture. Beat at medium speed for about 2 minutes. Gradually add $\frac{2}{3}$ cup of the remaining flour and the eggs. Beat at high speed for 2 minutes. Add the remaining flour and mix well. Cover and let rise until double in size. Beat the dough down on low speed and turn into the greased pan. Cover and let rise until increased in size by one-third to one-half (about 30 minutes). Bake in a 350°F oven for 40–50 minutes. (Hint: Use a stand mixer, not a hand mixer.)

Name: _____   Date: _____

Making Butter

When colonists ran out of butter, they didn't drive to the store and buy a couple of pounds. If they wanted butter, they either had to make it themselves or buy it from someone else in the colony.

Those who were lucky enough to have a cow were able to enjoy fresh butter, if they were willing to work a bit. Each day, a portion of the milk was set aside. When the creamy portion of the milk rose to the top, it was skimmed off and used to make butter.

Churning butter was a job often done by women or children. First, they poured fresh cream into a butter churn. Then they pushed the handle, called a dasher, up and down. Eventually, the cream turned into butter and buttermilk.

If you have a butter churn, you can make butter the old-fashioned way. If not, try this method.

Directions:
- Pour 1 cup of room-temperature whipping cream into a clear plastic container with a tight-fitting lid.
- Add 3 or 4 well-washed marbles and close tightly.
- Shake the jar continuously until butter forms. You may want to work with a partner or two, so your arms don't get tired.
- When butter forms, pour off the liquid. (This is buttermilk.)
- Remove the marbles.
- Rinse the butter with water to remove any excess liquid.
- Knead the butter with a spatula to bring together the curds.
- You can mix a little salt with the butter, and then put it into the refrigerator to cool and harden.

Graphic Organizer

Directions: Compare the taste of the butter you made with butter and margarine you purchase from a grocery store. Use the chart below to record your responses.

	Your Butter	**Store Butter**	**Store Margarine**
Taste			
Smell			
Color			
Firmness			
Which one do you like best? Why?			

Name: _____ Date: _____

Preserving Food

The colonists faced many challenges in the New World. One of those challenges was to preserve fruits, vegetables, and meat. Without refrigeration, food spoiled quickly, especially in warm weather.

The colonists used several methods to preserve food. Root cellars kept fruits and vegetables cool during the summer without allowing them to freeze in the winter. Food could also be stored inside crocks in a stream or well to keep it cool in summer. Meat and fish kept longer when smoked—cooked slowly over a fire. The colonists made jams, preserves, and jellies from berries and other fruit. Some types of fruit, vegetables, herbs, meat, and fish could be dried in the sun for several days during the summer and stored for use in winter. Dried beef turns into jerky. Raisins are dried grapes. Pickling was another way to preserve foods like cucumbers, onions, beets, and cabbages. When cabbage is pickled, it becomes sauerkraut.

Activity

Directions: Several types of snack foods include dried fruit. Today, we can use a microwave to dry fruit. With adult supervision, try drying apples using these instructions for the microwave.

1. Wash the apple and dry it off.

2. Remove the apple core.

3. Slice the apple as thinly as you possibly can.

4. Put the apple slices on a plain white paper towel. Cover them with another paper towel. The paper towels will absorb some of the excess juice from the apples.

5. Put the apple slices and towels on a microwave-safe shallow dish. Place the dish in the microwave.

6. Set the microwave to defrost or to 30% power.

7. Cook the apples for ten minutes.

8. Let the apple slices cool and put them in a plastic container. Do not cover the container.

9. Let the apples set in a dry place for a day.

UNIT TWO: THE COLONIES

Name: _____ Date: _____

Colonial Tools

Directions: Match the descriptions of the tools with the illustrations.

A.

____ 1. A thick-walled cooking pot with a tight-fitting lid that had a lip designed to hold hot coals was called a **dutch oven**.

B.

____ 2. Hot coals were put inside this **iron**. When hot, women used it to smooth wrinkles from clothes.

C.

____ 3. To warm a cold bed at night, colonists filled a **warming pan** with hot coals and moved it between the covers.

D.

____ 4. A **goffer** was used to iron bows and frills on hats and collars.

____ 5. Farmers used a long-handled **hay fork** to gather up straw or hay.

E.

____ 6. Metalworkers used **tongs** to hold hot metal.

F.

____ 7. Woodworkers used a **drawknife** to shape wood by shaving off thin layers.

G.

____ 8. Women used a **hackle** to comb knots from wool and make long threads.

H.

____ 9. To clean carpets, people used a **rug beater**.

I.

Name: _____ Date: _____

Learning About New Foods

When the colonists arrived in America, they learned to grow and eat many new foods. Some crops like corn, potatoes, and squash had grown only in the New World up to this time.

Corn was one of the most important crops colonists learned to grow. Corn on the cob could be roasted or boiled. Shelled corn was ground to make corn cakes or corn mush. Corn husks were used to stuff mattresses, make dolls, and were braided for mats. But best of all, corn could be popped.

Long before the colonists arrived, Native Americans enjoyed fresh, hot popcorn. They introduced this treat to early colonists. Many believe it was one of the foods eaten at the first Thanksgiving in 1621.

Although most varieties of corn look similar, only one type pops. What makes it pop? Water. In fact, each kernel explodes when the small amount of moisture inside is heated. The heat produces steam, and the pressure of the steam inside the corn causes the outside to burst open.

At first people cooked popcorn over glowing coals, but most of the kernels burned. They found they could lay stones on a hot fire and place the kernels on top of the stones to heat them. Fewer kernels burnt, but people were kept quite busy chasing the exploding kernels!

Later, people invented a wire basket to hold the kernels and the popped corn as they cooked it over an open fire. Popping corn in a closed kettle in oil became the standard method for over 100 years. Today, many people enjoy the quickness and convenience of microwave popcorn.

Research

Directions: The Columbian Exchange refers to the transfer of human populations, foods, animals, diseases, and ideas between the Eastern and Western Hemispheres. Research the origins of each item listed below and write on the blank next to it if it originated in the Americas (**Am**), Europe (**E**), or Asia (**As**).

_____ 1. beans   _____ 2. chocolate   _____ 3. chili peppers   _____ 4. silk

_____ 5. oxen   _____ 6. squash   _____ 7. cow   _____ 8. avocado

_____ 9. turkey   _____ 10. rice   _____ 11. sheep   _____ 12. horse

_____ 13. tomato   _____ 14. wheat   _____ 15. cloves   _____ 16. grapes

_____ 17. olives   _____ 18. potato   _____ 19. pig   _____ 20. nutmeg

Recycling Was a Way of Life

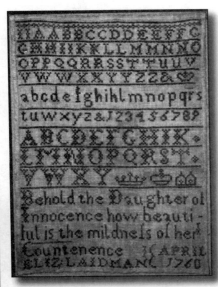

"Waste not, want not." This old saying was very much a part of daily colonial life. Little was wasted. At the end of the week, the colonists didn't set several plastic bags of garbage out by the street. In fact, they had very little garbage.

Almost every item the colonists had was useful for something. The hides of cows, oxen, goats, and other animals were also used to make leather. Furs from some animals were cured to make clothing, hats, mittens, or blankets. Food scraps and eggshells were fed to the animals or buried in the garden for fertilizer. Old clothing was reused to make another garment, sewn into quilts, or braided to make rag rugs. Corn husks were used to make dolls, as stuffing for mattresses, and were braided into baskets or floor mats. Flour sacks were made into clothing, dish towels, or curtains. Animal fat and grease were used to make soap and candles. Ashes were also an ingredient in soapmaking. Pillows and mattresses were stuffed with chicken, duck, and goose feathers. Feathers were also used for quill pens.

Colonists said that when they butchered a pig, they used everything except the oink. Besides ham, bacon, pork chops, and roast, people ate pickled pigs' feet, used the skin to make a soft leather, the fat to make tallow, the intestines to make sausage casings, and the bristles to make hair brushes.

When you consider how much they recycled or reused, you can understand why the colonists had little garbage at the end of a week.

Activity

1. Does your family recycle as well as the colonists did? _____

2. List ways you and your family reuse and recycle at home. _____

_____

_____

_____

_____

_____

_____

_____

Name: _____ Date: _____

The First Thanksgiving

Giving thanks for a bountiful harvest began long before the Pilgrims landed in the New World. The ancient Egyptians, Chinese, Greeks, and Romans all held fall festivals. People in Europe enjoyed feasting, dancing, and playing games at harvest festivals following the grain harvest.

The first American Thanksgiving, three days of prayer and feasting, was celebrated by the Plymouth colonists in 1621 to give thanks for their first harvest. The first settlers knew little about surviving in the wilderness. Half of them died during that first terrible winter in Massachusetts. The others survived only with the assistance of Native Americans.

When the Pilgrims planned their first thanksgiving festival, they prepared food for themselves and their ten expected guests. According to legend, nearly 90 Native Americans arrived. However, Chief Massasoit's hunters brought venison, insuring plenty of food for all.

The date of this thanksgiving festival is unknown, as are many details of what they did and ate. The menu probably included wild turkey, corn, fish, fruit, and venison. The next year the harvest was poor. A second thanksgiving festival wasn't held until 1623.

The custom of holding a thanksgiving festival spread as the colonies grew, but no single date was set. Some places celebrated in October, some in November. Even within the same settlement, the date changed from year to year.

The First Thanksgiving
by Jean Louis Gerome

President George Washington proclaimed November 26, 1789, as the first national Thanksgiving holiday, but various communities continued to celebrate Thanksgiving on different days.

In 1863, Sarah Hale persuaded President Abraham Lincoln to declare Thanksgiving as an annual national holiday held on the last Thursday in November. Many people objected when Franklin D. Roosevelt moved Thanksgiving to the third Thursday in November in 1939, to give people more time for Christmas shopping. Of the 48 states, 23 continued to observe the fourth Thursday and 23 celebrated on the earlier date. Two states, Texas and Colorado, celebrated Thanksgiving on both days. In 1941, Congress changed the date back to the fourth Thursday, and there it has remained.

UNIT TWO: THE COLONIES

Extension

Directions: On another sheet of paper, write a dialogue that might have taken place on the first Thanksgiving between a pilgrim and a Native American guest. Share your dialogue with the class.

Name: _____   Date: _____

Candlemaking

Without electricity, colonists relied on firelight, candles, and lanterns as sources of light.

They made candles by dipping a wick made of flax or cotton fibers into melted wax or fat, removing it, and letting it cool. The hot wax adhered to the wick and became hard when it cooled. Candles were made thicker by dipping them into the melted wax several times.

Imagine what a candle made from animal fat would smell like when it burned! Herbs, spices, or dried flower petals could be added when candles were made to make them smell better. The most expensive candles were made from beeswax.

Did You Know?

The nursery rhyme "Jack Be Nimble" is based on a game children played while their parents made candles. After dipping candles, colonial women hung them from two long horizontal sticks to allow them to harden and cool. These sticks, and not the candles themselves, were the "candlesticks" Jack jumped over.

Extension

Directions: Write a short rhyme similar to "Jack Be Nimble," based on any aspect of colonial life.

_____

_____

_____

_____

_____

_____

_____

_____

UNIT TWO: THE COLONIES

Name: _____   Date: _____

Soapmaking

Bathing with soap and water and washing clothes were not items high on the list of priorities for the colonists. It wasn't uncommon for people to wear the same clothes every day for a month or more and bathe even less frequently.

The recipe for making soap is a simple one: lye + water + fat = soap. The process of making soap wasn't quite so simple; it took most of a day to make one barrel of soap and was done outdoors because of the strong smells and mess involved. Colonists usually only made soap once or twice a year.

To make soap, the colonists first prepared tallow. They hung a large kettle over an outdoor fire and filled it with cooking grease and animal fat they had saved. It took about 20 to 25 pounds of fat and grease to make one barrel of soap.

The fat and grease then had to be rendered to produce tallow. Tallow was used in both soap and candlemaking. This process involved cooking the fat and grease with water and then skimming off the grease that floated to the top. The grease was strained to remove impurities. This sometimes had to be done two or three times before the tallow could be used.

To obtain lye, they poured hot water through a tub called a leach barrel filled with ashes. The water filtered through the ashes out a hole in the barrel, forming lye. It took five or six large buckets of ashes to produce enough lye for one barrel of soap.

Working with lye is dangerous because it can cause terrible burns to the skin or eyes. Fumes can burn the lungs. If swallowed, it is poisonous.

Lye and tallow were then mixed together in the kettle with water and boiled until they formed a jelly-like substance. This substance, called soft soap, was stored in a barrel and used as needed.

UNIT TWO: THE COLONIES

Fill in the Blanks

1. The recipe for making soap is _____ + _____ + fat = soap.

2. To make soap, the colonists first prepared _____.

3. To obtain lye, they poured hot water through a tub called a leach barrel filled with _____.

4. Working with lye is dangerous because it can cause terrible _____ to the skin or eyes. Fumes can burn the _____. If swallowed, it is _____.

5. Lye and tallow were mixed together in the kettle with water and boiled until they formed a jelly-like substance called _____ _____.

Think About It

If people still had to carry all the water for every bath into the house in buckets, heat it on the stove, dump it into the bathtub, and take a bath in an unheated room, how often do you think they would bathe?

Name: _____ Date: _____

Dyeing for Color

Not only did most of the colonists have to spin thread, weave their own fabrics, and sew their own clothes, they also had to dye the fabrics if they wanted colors. By using plants that grew in their gardens or in the woods, they were able to produce many different colors.

- A strong tea solution is used for brown.
- The dry skins of yellow onions make a yellow dye.
- Strawberries or raspberries produce pink.
- Blueberries and purple grapes make a blue or purple dye.
- Spinach produces green dye.
- The pulp of grated beets can be used for red.

Cooperative Learning

Directions: Work as a group. Each member should dye three strips of fabric in three different colors. This can be a messy project. Be sure to protect your work area with newspapers, a tarp, or an old plastic tablecloth. Wear old clothes or an apron.

1. Cut strips of white fabric about 2 inches wide and 2 feet long. Only natural fabrics like cotton or wool will work. An old white T-shirt can be used if it is 100% cotton.

2. Make your dyes in large plastic bowls. Label the bowls #1, #2, and #3. Pour hot water over the plants you use. Let the bowls sit overnight.

3. Remove the plant products before adding fabric.

4. Wet the fabric thoroughly before dyeing.

5. Stir the fabric in the dye so the color is even. The longer the fabric stays in the dye, the darker it will be.

6. Wring out the fabric completely when finished, then rinse it in cold water to set the color.

7. Hang the fabric to dry.

8. Use your results to complete the following chart.

	Bowl 1	Bowl 2	Bowl 3
Plant Used			
Color Produced			

UNIT TWO: THE COLONIES

Name: _____ Date: _____

Colonial Quilts

Colonial women made quilts by hand-sewing pieces of fabric together to form a design. The fabric was cut from different pieces of old or outgrown clothing. They attached a backing and stuffed the middle with a soft material such as cotton, goose down, or wool. To keep the stuffing in place, they sewed through all three layers, usually in a decorative pattern.

Because sewing materials were scarce and women had few outlets for artistic expression, quilts became a way to create something beautiful as well as practical. Quiltmakers displayed their work at fairs, and prizes were given for original designs. Quilts were often given as gifts for weddings or other special occasions.

Besides being beautiful, quilts had a very practical purpose: they helped keep people warm on cold winter nights.

Making a large quilt took many hours. Sometimes several women got together for a "quilting bee." They all made individual squares and then sewed the squares together to make the finished quilt. Quilting bees helped women finish their quilts more quickly and gave them an opportunity to sit with their friends and visit while they worked.

UNIT TWO: THE COLONIES

Think About It
Many of the quilts made were called "patchwork" quilts. Why do you think this term was used?

Cooperative Learning

Directions: Hold a quilting bee. Each person in the group can make one or more paper quilt squares. You can use a popular quilt square pattern or make up your own.

1. For each quilt square, cut a piece of graph paper into an eight- or nine-inch square. (Make sure everyone in the group makes the same size square.)

2. Draw your design on the graph paper.

3. You may color in the design or cut and glue paper to fit the design on the graph paper. You may use items such as wallpaper scraps, color ads from magazines, scrapbook paper, or wrapping paper for your pattern pieces.

4. When finished, glue the quilt squares on a large piece of colored kraft or butcher paper. Be sure to keep the rows and columns even. Display the finished quilt for everyone to enjoy.

Name: _____   Date: _____

From Wool to Clothing

In spring, colonists sheared sheep. The heavy winter wool they cut from the animals could be turned into clothing for the colonists—with a bit of work.

When first cut, wool is oily, dirty, and matted. Sticks, leaves, and burrs had to be removed from the tangled **fleece**. The wool was then washed and carded. Carding means to fluff and straighten the fibers.

Spinning is the process of making yarn or thread from a fiber, such as wool, cotton, flax, or **jute**. Colonists used a spinning wheel and a distaff—a stick that held a bundle of the fiber for spinning. A foot pedal turned the wheel joining the fibers into a continuous length for use in weaving or knitting. Wool was dyed either before or after spinning.

The next step was to weave the yarn on a loom to make cloth. The cloth could then be cut and sewn to make clothing.

Did You Know? Cloth woven from flax fiber is called linen.

Activity

Directions: Complete the vocabulary chart by creating a definition, using the word in a sentence, and drawing an illustration that helps you remember the meaning of the word.

Word	Definition	Illustration
fleece		
	Sentence	
Word	Definition	Illustration
jute		
	Sentence	

Name: _____ Date: _____

Weaving

When the colonists arrived, many brought their looms. Some looms were so large, they took up almost an entire room. Many women learned basic weaving, while skilled artisans wove complex, beautiful designs.

Weaving is the process of interlacing pliable materials, usually at right angles to each other. Cloth is woven from yarn. Weaving can be quite simple or very complex, depending on the materials used and the size, shape, and pattern desired. Baskets can be woven from various plant materials such as reeds or vines. Other materials can be used for weaving mats and rugs.

Activity

Directions: To understand weaving, create a simple design with strips of colored construction paper. For more complicated designs, you can use more than two colors or paper strips in varying widths.

Materials for simple paper weaving:
 Ten 12″ x 1″ strips of dark-colored construction paper
 Twenty 12″ x $\frac{1}{2}$″ strips of light-colored construction paper
 One 10″ x 10″ piece of cardboard
 Clear or masking tape

1. Place the dark-colored strips side-by-side across the cardboard. Do not allow the strips to overlap. Turn over the one-inch overhang on both ends. Tape ends securely to the back of the cardboard.

2. Turn the cardboard 90°.

3. Begin the first row by weaving a light-colored strip over the first dark strip, under the second, over, under, etc.

4. Tape the one-inch overhang on both ends of the light-colored strip to the back of the cardboard.

5. Begin the second row by weaving another light-colored strip next to the first one. This time go under the first dark strip, over the second, under, over, etc. Tape ends as before.

6. Repeat steps 3 to 5 until all light-colored strips are used.

Name: _____ Date: _____

Make a Sampler

Girls as young as five or six were taught to make samplers. Making a sampler served more than one purpose. Since many girls did not have an opportunity to go to school, they learned the alphabet while they learned to sew.

A young girl's first sampler project might be to embroider a long piece of linen with the letters of the alphabet drawn on by an adult. Older girls embroidered samplers with the multiplication tables, pictures, or words to Bible verses.

As they gained experience, women's samplers might contain elaborate pictures of flowers and animals. Finished samplers were used as wall hangings or pillow covers. Combining several different stitches and colors of thread added texture and made samplers more interesting. Three common stitches are shown at the right.

chain stitch

cross-stitch

stem or outline stitch

Extension

Directions: Try making your own sampler.

1. Practice making the three types of stitches shown. Use a white or light-colored washcloth for material.

2. Thread a darning needle with yarn and make a knot at the end. Practice one type of stitch at a time. When you finish, tie off the yarn on the back of the washcloth.

3. After you've practiced each type of stitch, cut and remove the practice stitches.

4. Make a simple sampler by neatly printing your name with chalk in large block letters. Use any of the stitches you practiced or a combination of them to embroider your name. You can add flowers, animals, or other designs to your sampler to make it more elaborate.

5. If you like your sampler, you can frame it and hang it for a decoration.

Name: _____ Date: _____

Make a Whirligig

One of the homemade toys children in the colonies played with was a whirligig. In colonial times, a whirligig might have been made by cutting a thin slice of wood from a three- to four-inch diameter tree branch and using a nail to punch the center holes.

Activity

Directions: Make a whirligig.

1. Use the pattern below to cut a circle from heavy cardboard.

2. Punch holes in the center as shown on the pattern.

3. Use markers to create a colorful geometric design on both sides of the circle. (Spirals or concentric circles look great.)

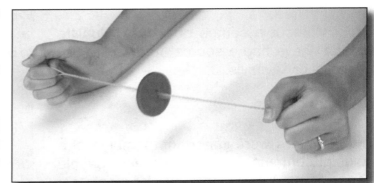

4. Thread about $2\frac{1}{2}$ feet of string through the holes, and tie the ends together.

5. Hold the string between the thumb and index finger of both hands. Twirl until the string is tight.

6. Stretch out the string to make the whirligig spin. By pulling and relaxing the tension on the string, you can keep it going for quite a while. Hold contests to see who can keep the whirligig spinning the longest.

7. Listen as the whirligig spins. Why do you think it's called a whirligig?

   _____
   _____
   _____
   _____
   _____

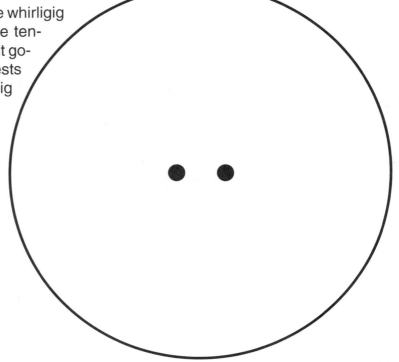

UNIT TWO: THE COLONIES

The Importance of Water

Having a nearby source of fresh water was critical to the colonists. It was needed for cooking, drinking, watering crops, feeding livestock, bathing, and putting out fires. Metalworkers needed water to cool items they made. Papermakers needed water to make paper. Water was also a major means of transportation.

Without a source of water, colonists wouldn't have had a source of power to run gristmills or sawmills.

Gristmill

Millers were important members of a colonial community. To make bread, people needed flour. Wheat, corn, rye, and oats are tough grains that must be ground to produce flour or meal. Grinding grain by hand is a very difficult job. When enough settlers lived in an area, they built a gristmill. Farmers would travel many miles to have their grain made into flour or meal.

The gristmill needed power to move the machinery used to grind grain. Without electricity, the power needed was usually provided by moving water. Gristmills were built beside streams or rivers. A dam built across the stream created a millpond. The millpond provided a steady flow of water to the waterwheel, which used gears to turn a millstone and grind the grain. As the millstone turned, the grain was crushed into finer particles to make flour or meal.

Sawmill

If colonists wanted wooden planks before sawmills were built, they had to chop down trees and cut the logs into boards. People who sawed the planks from the logs were called **sawyers**. They used a broadax to square up logs or a two-person whipsaw to make planks. Producing one plank required much time and energy, and they needed hundreds of boards to build one house. Without a sawmill, building a house, barn, or other structure was a major undertaking. That's why many of the early buildings were made of logs.

Sawmills, like gristmills, depended on water power. Water power could also be used to transport logs from where they were cut downstream to the sawmill.

Once a sawmill was built in a settlement, the village tended to grow more quickly. People moved to areas with sawmills because they could build houses and shops more easily. More people and available lumber encouraged woodworkers like carpenters, cabinetmakers, coopers, wheelwrights, and wainwrights to set up shops nearby.

Name: _____   Date: _____

The Importance of Water (cont.)

Critical Thinking

Do you think water is more or less important to a community today than it was in colonial times? Give specific details or examples to support your answer.

_____

_____

_____

_____

_____

Graphic Organizer

Directions: Complete the vocabulary chart by creating a definition, using the word in a sentence, and drawing an illustration that helps you remember the meaning of the word.

Word	Definition	Illustration
miller		
	Sentence	
Word	Definition	Illustration
sawyer		
	Sentence	

Research

Directions: Learn more about how a gristmill worked. Draw a diagram on a separate sheet of paper to show how a waterwheel, gears, and millstone were used to grind grain.

Name: _____ Date: _____

Coopers

Do you know anyone whose last name is Cooper? Chances are, one of that person's ancestors was a real **cooper**—a person who made wooden barrels, buckets, pails, tubs, and piggins. A **piggin** was a small wooden pail with one stave extended above the rim to serve as a handle. Colonists used these containers to store everything from nails to pickles to eggs. A good barrel had to be watertight and could be used to store liquids.

A cooper made a barrel by binding wooden planks, called **staves**, together with wooden or metal **hoops**. Staves were carved from large pieces of oak, pine, or cedar and shaped so they were wider in the middle and narrower at the ends.

tops and bottoms of barrels were cut from wide planks of wood. A hole in the top of the barrel allowed liquids to be poured in or out of the barrel. A tightfitting wooden peg was used to close the hole to prevent spilling or evaporation.

The cooper used a **trussing ring** to hold the staves upright in a circle, while he pulled them tightly together using a rope, crank, and **windlass** (winch).

Then the cooper placed hoops around the staves to keep everything in place. The

---

Did You Know?
Ships sailing between England and the New World were required by law to have at least one master cooper as part of the crew. His job was to oversee barrels containing water and other provisions and to prevent any of the barrels from leaking.

Critical Thinking

Why do you think coopers made staves in the shape they did? Give specific details or examples to support your opinion.

_____

_____

_____

_____

_____

_____

_____

UNIT TWO: THE COLONIES

Name: _____ Date: _____

Cabinetmakers

"All the countrey is overgrowne with trees ..." wrote Captain John Smith when he came to Jamestown in 1607. Trees were one of the most valuable resources the colonists found in the New World.

In colonial times, all furniture was made by hand. Most people learned to make some of their own furniture, like tables, chairs, benches, and bed frames. The furniture they made was strong, heavy, and practical but, for the most part, not very beautiful. Many people did not have the skills, time, or tools to make fine furniture. That work was done by cabinetmakers.

Cabinetmakers created many elegant pieces of furniture held together without glue or nails. This was done by hand carving precise joints that fit together perfectly. Sometimes cabinetmakers were called joiners, because they were experts at connecting pieces of wood in ways that were strong, neat, and almost invisible.

Cabinetmakers used many hand tools in their work including saws, hammers, drills, mallets, planes, chisels, knives, and **lathes**. To give furniture a beautiful finish, the cabinetmaker used stain, vegetable dye, oil, or varnish. Polishing and rubbing in the finish was a job often done by the cabinetmaker's apprentice. Besides making fine furniture, cabinetmakers also made and repaired musical instruments, repaired furniture, and even made coffins.

Did You Know?
Since the cabinetmaker made coffins, he often took care of funeral arrangements as well.

UNIT TWO: THE COLONIES

 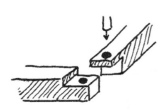 

dovetail joint   **lap joint**   **mortise and tenon**   **tongue and groove**

Research

Directions: Use reference sources to learn more about the craft of woodworking. Use the information to answer the questions below.

1. What is a lathe? _____
_____

2. What does a woodworker use a lathe for? _____
_____
_____

Name: _____ Date: _____

Wheelwrights

Colonists needed wagons and carts for transportation and to haul goods. Since wheels were made of wood and roads were rough and bumpy, wheels needed frequent repair. Wheelwrights made and repaired wooden wheels.

To make a wooden wheel, the wheelwright started with the **hub**. This was the center of a wheel and needed to be the strongest part. It was made from very hard wood, aged for several years. **Spokes** were attached to the hub to give the rim strength. The axle, made of cast iron, ran through the center of the hub. The **rim** of the wheel was made of curved sections of wood called felloes, joined to make a full circle.

To finish a wheel, an **iron ring**, slightly smaller than the rim, was heated so it would expand enough to fit tightly around the rim. The wheelwright then hammered the iron ring onto the rim while it was still hot. When it cooled, the iron ring contracted and fit tightly around the rim.

Diagram

Directions: Label the hub, spokes, rim, and iron ring on this wheel.

A. _____   B. _____

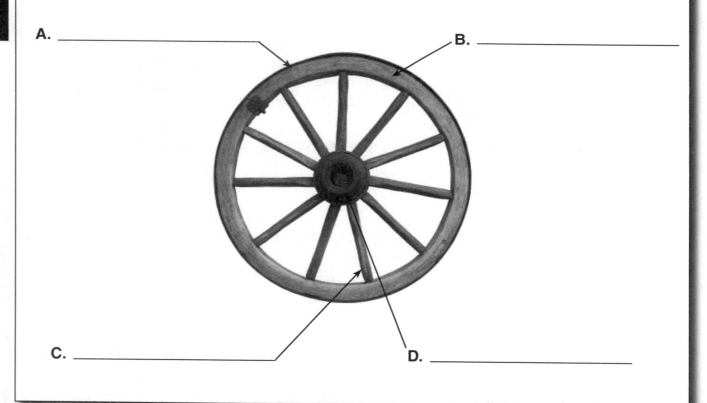

C. _____   D. _____

Name: _____ Date: _____

Blacksmiths

When people picture a blacksmith from the colonial period, they often think of a person making horseshoes. Making shoes for horses and oxen was part of a blacksmith's job but a minor one. The blacksmith created fireplace and kitchen utensils, kettles, guns, pots and pans, metal hoops for barrels, and farm tools. He also made latches, locks, and nails.

The blacksmith worked at a raised brick hearth called a forge. A coal fire provided the heat needed to make iron soft enough to bend. He used a large bellows to fan the flames and keep the fire hot.

Blacksmiths used other tools in their work, including tongs to hold the hot metal, hammers to pound metal into the desired shape, and an anvil, which was a large, cast-iron block. The blacksmith hammered his pieces into shape on the anvil. To change the shape of iron, the blacksmith heated it until it became **malleable** and then hammered it on the anvil.

During the Revolutionary War, black-smiths were kept very busy making cannons, cannon balls, and other tools of war. The Continental Congress hired Peter Townsend, a blacksmith, to make a huge iron chain long enough to stretch across the narrow part of the Hudson River near West Point to stop British warships. Each link of the chain was about one foot by three feet. In all, it measured about 500 yards. Held in place by iron anchors, which Townsend also made, the chain did its job. No British warships were able to sail past it.

> **Did You Know?**
> The word *smith* comes from *smite* (to hit or pound something). A blacksmith worked mostly with iron, which is black. So the word *blacksmith* means "a person who pounds black metal."

Graphic Organizer

Directions: Complete the vocabulary chart by creating a definition, using the word in a sentence, and drawing an illustration that helps you remember the meaning of the word.

Word	Definition	Illustration
malleable		
	Sentence	

Name: _____ Date: _____

Pewterers and Silversmiths

Once colonists had most of the necessities they needed for daily life, they also wanted items that were decorative and beautiful.

People who worked as **pewterers** and **silversmiths** were artisans. They poured hot, melted metal into molds formed in the shape of the item they wished to produce: shoe buckles, buttons, candleholders, dishes, spoons, cups, and teapots. Silversmiths worked with gold, brass, and copper as well as silver.

Paul Revere was one of the best known silversmiths during the colonial period. He was born in Boston in 1735. The son of a silversmith, he became a silversmith and engraver. He was well known during his lifetime as a designer of elegant silverware, tankards, bowls, plates, pitchers, and tea sets. He also designed the first seal for the united colonies as well as the seal still used by Massachusetts.

> **Did You Know?**
> Paul Revere also made artificial teeth, surgical instruments, engraved printing plates, and printed money for the Massachusetts Congress.

Graphic Organizer

Directions: Compare and contrast the trade of pewterers and silversmiths. Complete the Venn diagram below.

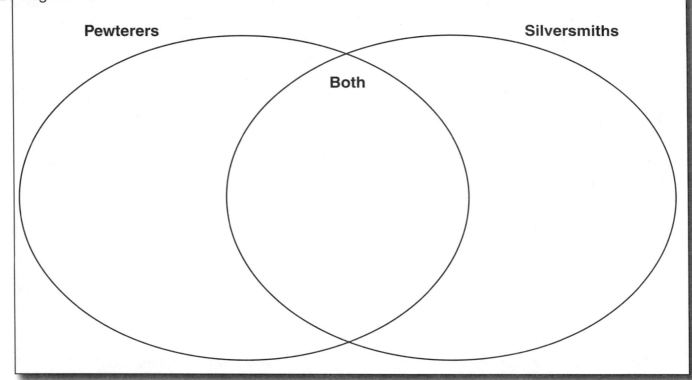

Name: _____ Date: _____

Tinsmiths

Tin is a soft, silvery metal used to make pails, lanterns, and kitchen utensils. A **tinsmith** hammered sheets of tin into useful shapes. He also made and repaired lightweight pots and pans. Records show that Paul Revere, a silversmith, also made **tinware**.

Decorative tinware was one of the arts practiced in colonial times. Designs were punched or pierced into a piece of tin in decorative patterns. Tinsmiths cut the tin to shape and then embossed a pattern on it by gently striking a punch with a hammer to form depressions in the tin.

Sheets of tin that were decorated with a punched design were often placed in the doors and sides of cabinets called **pie safes**. Food could be placed inside the cabinet to keep it safe from insects and mice, while the small holes in the tin allowed air to circulate.

Activity

Directions: To make tin-punch art, you will need a square of heavy cardboard, a piece of aluminum foil larger than the cardboard, tape, a two- to three-inch finishing nail (one with a small, rounded top), graph paper, and a pencil.

1. Cover the cardboard with the aluminum foil, wrapping the excess around the back.

2. Smooth the aluminum foil, and use tape on the back to hold it firmly in place.

3. Draw a design on graph paper the same size as your cardboard. Place the graph paper drawing over the foil and cardboard. Use the top of the nail to impress the design on the aluminum-covered cardboard. Press firmly to indent the design but not so hard that you rip the foil.

Name: _____   Date: _____

Printers

Printing is a method of pressing letters, words, sentences, and pictures onto sheets of paper. Whether they printed their own words or the words of others, **printers** (those who ran printing presses) influenced the thoughts and opinions of their fellow colonists.

The Reverend Jose Glover, the first printer to sail for the New World, never arrived. He and Stephen Daye, a blacksmith hired to accompany him, loaded up the printing equipment and supplies and sailed from England with their families. However, Glover died at sea.

The families settled in Cambridge, Massachusetts, and Mrs. Glover hired Stephen Daye to open a print shop. At that time, the political and religious leaders of the colony controlled everything that was printed. If they didn't approve, the printer could be arrested, fined, and put out of business.

The first item Daye printed in 1639 was "The Free-Man's Oath," a statement of allegiance that all colonists were required to sign.

In 1640, Daye printed *The Whole Booke of Psalmes,* the first full-length book published in the New World.

Other printers set up shops in the colonies, but problems quickly arose because printers wanted to print whatever they wished. *Publick Occurrences,* the first newspaper printed in Boston in 1690, was shut down after one issue because it criticized the British in their war with the French.

John Peter Zenger, editor of the *New-York Weekly Journal,* was arrested in 1735 for printing articles criticizing the government. His lawyer argued that although he had broken the law, the fact that he had printed the truth was more important. The jury did not convict Zenger. From this case came the idea of "freedom of the press."

Critical Thinking

1. What does "freedom of the press" mean to you? Explain your answer by giving specific details or examples.

_____

_____

_____

_____

2. Do you think newspapers should always have the right to print anything they want if it's true? Support your opinion with specific details or examples.

_____

_____

_____

Name: _____   Date: _____

Apprentices

In colonial times, there were no factories to produce goods. If a person needed a saddle, barrel, candlestick, wheel, or nail, someone had to make it. Specialists, called **masters**, in many trades produced these items.

People did not learn their jobs by attending schools. Sometimes children learned skills from their parents. Another way was for children between the ages of seven and 15 to become **apprentices**. Since women rarely worked outside their homes, most apprentices were boys.

At the end of the apprenticeship, each person was required to produce a finished object called a **masterpiece**. If the object was good enough, the apprentice became a journeyman. The term *journeyman* came about because after completing their apprenticeships, many young men journeyed around the country, making and repairing goods until they saved enough money to open their own shops.

Did You Know?

When Benjamin Franklin was 15, his father apprenticed him to his older brother James, a printer.

A formal apprenticeship usually lasted between four and seven years. During that time, the master provided room, board, clothing, and training. In exchange for their training, apprentices worked hard without pay. They ran errands, did chores around the house or shop, and helped the master at his trade.

This system was very practical at the time and worked well if the master craftsman was a good person and skilled in his trade. Problems arose if the master was cruel and lazy.

UNIT TWO: THE COLONIES

Activity

Directions: Compare today's education system to the apprentice system. Make a study aid to display your information.

1. Fold a sheet of white paper in half lengthwise like a hotdog bun.
2. Fold the paper in half again, from side to side.
3. Unfold the paper and cut up the fold, making two flaps.
4. On the front of one flap, write *Advantages of Apprentice System*. On the other flap, write *Advantages of Today's System*. Under the flaps, list three advantages of each system.

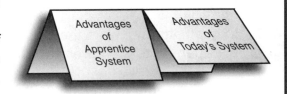

Name: _____ Date: _____

Colonial Education

As colonial settlements grew, the people built schools for their children. Most schools contained only one room with wooden desks. One teacher taught all the children from first through eighth grades. Older students helped teach younger ones.

Teachers were paid by members of the community, sometimes in money, but more often in goods and services. Families took turns providing room and board for the teacher.

Children learned the "three R's" in school—reading, (w)riting, and (a)rithmetic.

Schools had very few books and maps, no libraries, and of course, no media center. **Hornbooks** were used by children to help them learn to read. A hornbook was a page of writing covered with a translucent (see-through) sheet of animal horn fastened to a wooden frame. Twine or rope was threaded through a hole in the handle, making it easy for students to hang the hornbooks around their necks or fasten them to their belts.

At first, paper was too expensive to use except for very special letters and documents. Instead, children wrote on small pieces of slate with chalk or slate pencils. The advantage of this method was that the slates could be wiped clean and reused over and over.

Activity

Directions: Make a hornbook.

1. Cut out the hornbook shape from a piece of heavy brown cardboard.

2. Punch a hole in the handle.

3. Thread a 12-inch length of yarn through the hole and tie the ends.

4. Cut a sheet of plain white paper to fit on the hornbook.

5. In neat lettering, write the capital letters of the alphabet on the top half of the white sheet of paper. Write the lower-case letters on the bottom half of the sheet.

6. Glue the paper to one side of the hornbook.

Name: _____   Date: _____

Make a Quill Pen

The colonists used quill pens and ink to write their letters and important documents. Quill pens were made from the wing or tail feathers of geese, turkeys, and other large birds. Thomas Jefferson wrote the Declaration of Independence using a quill pen.

> **Did You Know?**
> Both the Declaration of Independence and the Constitution were written using ink and a quill pen.

Activity

Directions: Make your own quill pen and ink by following these steps.

1. Soak a large feather (about 10 inches long) in warm soapy water for 15 minutes. Dry it with a paper towel.

2. Cut off the bottom two inches of the tip with scissors. Cut at an angle. This is the point of the pen called the nib.

3. Use a pin or toothpick to carefully clean out the center of the nib.

4. Cut a small slit in the nib. This helps control the flow of ink.

5. Make ink by crushing one cup of berries through a strainer into a glass jar. Add 1 teaspoon of vinegar and one teaspoon of salt. If the ink is too pale, add a drop of red or blue food coloring.

   CAUTION: Cover your work area with newspapers. Do not spill ink on your clothes. It may leave a permanent stain.

6. To write, tip the nib into the ink. Press off the excess ink on a paper towel. Hold the quill at an angle, and write with the tip. Repeat this step when your pen runs out of ink.

7. Use your quill pen and ink to sign your name in large letters like John Hancock did on the Declaration of Independence.

Name: _____ Date: _____

Colonial Word Search

Directions: Look up, down, backward, forward, and diagonally to find the 40 words hidden in the puzzle that have to do with colonial people, jobs, foods, tools, trades, and crafts.

```
D G Y K B H T H G I R W L E E H W E L K H V G N
H S W X S L C L S D Y M T R E C Y C L E D P F L
Z A F D L N A C M E N Q K K J K K I Z C D W T J
G W R N V K I C R S C N V J K I B T K S R V T T
N Y P R R J L B K K A I D K Z T Y N N T Q Z Z L
I E B C W Z M T A S L M P G R C Z E F S R R T G
N R S K H I P E R C M O P S M H W R D I K V N Q
N T N E L C D V G S G I O L W E B P T N M I R M
I P M L I M R Y C G Q O T W E N C P Z O T D M R
P V E X W N H H Q H S B L H M R S A L L F G N T
S R R H T V O L R N P U V V W K R E I O N K V T
T W G T G O K L A Q J T P K R B E U S C X M Y H
Y O J L L L H S O B W T X Z R B Q T Q R T Y T W
G L K M D R I C L C N E P A O S N Y T N O I Z A
T P T Z N T A D B A R R E L S K C W T L M H R I
F P N T R N J E L L Y C O R N H U S K S E E P N
A G U A D T L L I M T S I R G Z C T N K P S C W
R K H L G X W Q W G Q C F N N R V I O O Q C X R
M K E L J N G E A G H M D D T P T M O Y G M N I
I S H C K T A M F F M J L N R U H C L N S X K G
N L D M M V E Z P H D K L M N M L M L N Y V K H
G P L Q E S T O O L S P A V N K R T J N E X O T
V G L N G L Q J P M T J W V F G N L T W Q G K Y
```

APPRENTICE	CORNHUSKS	KITCHEN	SOAP
ARTISANS	EGGS	LOG CABINS	SPICES
BARRELS	FARMING	MILLER	SPINNING
BLACKSMITH	GAMES	OXEN	TINSMITH
BUTTER	GRISTMILL	PLOW	TOOLS
CANDLES	HORSES	QUILTING	TOYS
CHURN	HUNT	RECYCLE	WAINWRIGHT
COLONIES	JAM	SAMPLER	WEAVE
COLONISTS	JELLY	SAWYER	WHEELWRIGHT
COOPER	KETTLES	SCHOOL	WOOL

Name: _____ Date: _____

Important Colonists

Research

Directions: Learn more about eight of the people from the list below who were important during the colonial period of American history. Using the information, create a graphic organizer to display your work.

Abigail Adams	Thomas Hooker	Chief Powhatan
Ann Austin	John Hull	Sir Walter Raleigh
John Billington	Anne Hutchinson	Paul Revere
William Bradford	Margaret Jones	John Rolfe
Anne Bradstreet	Captain William Kidd	Captain John Smith
Margaret Brent	Cotton Mather	Squanto
George Calvert	Increase Mather	Myles Standish
Rev. John Elliot	Peter Minuit	Peter Stuyvesant
Mary Fisher	James Ogelthorpe	Roger Williams
Benjamin Franklin	William Penn	Samuel Winslow
Patrick Henry	Pocahontas	John Winthrop

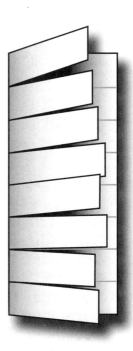

1. Fold a sheet of white unlined paper in half lengthwise like a hotdog bun.

2. Next, fold the paper in fourths and then in eighths.

3. Unfold the paper. You now have a hotdog bun folded in eight equal parts.

4. Form eight tabs by cutting from the edge of the paper to the main fold.

5. Write the name of a different colonist on each of the front tabs.

6. Behind the tabs, write an important contribution each of the colonists made to the American colonial era.

Time Line of the American Revolution

1733 • Molasses Act imposed taxes on molasses, rum, and sugar.

1754 • French and Indian War began.

1760 • George III became king of England.

1763 • Treaty of Paris ended French and Indian War.
     • Proclamation of 1763 forbade colonists to settle west of the Appalachian Mountains.

1764 • Sugar Act taxed colonists on lumber, molasses, rum, and other foods.
     • Currency Act prevented colonies from issuing their own money and devaluated colonial scrip.

1765 • Quartering Act required colonists to provide barracks and supplies for British troops.
     • Stamp Act required colonists to buy government stamps for documents, etc.
     • Stamp Act Congress pledged not to pay taxes unless approved by colonial legislatures.

1766 • Stamp Act repealed.
     • Declaratory Act gave Parliament the right to tax colonists.

1767 • Townshend Duties taxed colonists on glass, paper, and tea.

1770 • Boston Massacre.
     • Townshend Acts repealed, except tax on tea.

1773 • Tea Act gave British East India Company a monopoly on tea trade in the colonies.
     • Boston Tea Party.

1774 • Intolerable Acts closed the port of Boston and decreased powers of local authority.
     • British General Gage and troops arrived in Boston.
     • First Continental Congress met in Philadelphia.

1775 • **March 23:** Patrick Henry delivered "Give me liberty ..." speech.
     • **April 19:** Battles at Lexington and Concord.
     • **May 10:** Second Continental Congress met.
     • **June 10:** George Washington named commander in chief of Continental Army.
     • **June 17:** Battle at Breed's Hill.

1776 • **July 4:** Declaration of Independence approved.
     • **August 1:** British defeated at Charleston.
     • **August 27–29:** British defeated Washington in Battle of Long Island.
     • **September 6:** First submarine, the *Turtle,* failed to sink Admiral Howe's flagship.
     • **September 22:** Nathan Hale hanged as a spy.
     • **October 28:** Battle of White Plains.
     • **November 16:** British forces captured Fort Washington.
     • **December:** Benjamin Franklin arrived in France as U.S. envoy.
     • **December 19:** Thomas Paine published *The Crisis.*
     • **December 25–26:** Washington crossed the Delaware River and attacked the British at Trenton, New Jersey.

UNIT THREE: REVOLUTION & CONSTITUTION

Time Line of the American Revolution (cont.)

1777   • **January 3:** Washington drove the British from Princeton, New Jersey.
      • **June 14:** Congress authorized a United States flag.
      • **July:** The Vermont Constitution abolished slavery.
      • **July 6:** British recaptured Fort Ticonderoga.
      • **September 9–11:** Battle of Brandywine: British forced Washington's army back toward Philadelphia.
      • **September 26:** British captured Philadelphia.
      • **October 4–5:** British won Battle of Germantown.
      • **October 17:** Americans defeated British at Saratoga.
      • **November 15:** Continental Congress approved the Articles of Confederation.
      • **December 17:** Washington's army went into winter quarters at Valley Forge.

1778   • **February 6:** France signed Treaty of Alliance with the United States.
      • **June 27–28:** Battle of Monmouth.
      • **July 20:** American forces captured fort at Vincennes, Indiana.
      • **August 8:** Battle at Newport, Rhode Island.
      • **December 29:** British captured Savannah, Georgia.

1779   • **January 29:** British captured Augusta, Georgia.
      • **June 1:** British captured forts at Stony Point and Verplanck, New York.
      • **September 23:** John Paul Jones captured British warship, *Serapis.*
      • **September 27:** Congress appointed John Adams to negotiate peace with England.
      • **October 17:** Washington led troops to winter quarters in Morristown, New Jersey.

1780   • **May 12:** Charleston surrendered to the British.
      • **June 23:** British defeated at Battle of Springfield, New Jersey.
      • **September 8:** British forces began invading South Carolina.
      • **September 23–25:** Benedict Arnold revealed as a traitor.
      • **October 7:** American militia won at Kings Mountain, North Carolina.

1781   • **March 1:** Articles of Confederation ratified by all states.
      • **March 16:** British won the Battle of Guilford Courthouse.
      • **May 9:** British surrendered Pensacola, Florida, to Spanish.
      • **September 8:** American forces defeated at Eutaw Springs, South Carolina.
      • **October 19:** British surrendered at Yorktown.

1782   • **January:** Loyalists began leaving for Canada or England.
      • **April 12:** Peace talks between Great Britain and the United States began.
      • **October 8:** The United States and the Netherlands signed treaty of commerce and friendship.
      • **November 30:** Preliminary peace treaty signed between the United States and Great Britain.

1783   • **September 1:** Treaty of Paris signed.

1787   • **September 17:** Constitution of the United States signed.

1788   • **July:** Constitution ratified and goes into effect.

1791   • **December 15:** Bill of Rights approved as amendments to the Constitution.

Name: _____ Date: _____

American Revolution Time Line Activity

Directions: Use the information from the time line to answer the questions below.

Sequencing: Check the event in each group that came first.

1. _____ The French and Indian War ended.
   _____ George III became King of England.

2. _____ The Currency Act prevented colonists from issuing their own money.
   _____ Great Britain passed the Stamp Act.

3. _____ Boston Massacre
   _____ Boston Tea Party

4. _____ George Washington was named commander-in-chief of the Continental Army.
   _____ Battles were fought at Lexington and Concord.

5. _____ Declaration of Independence approved
   _____ Articles of Confederation approved

6. _____ Treaty of Paris ends Revolutionary War.
   _____ British surrendered at Yorktown.

7. _____ Townshend Acts repealed
   _____ Stamp Act repealed

8. _____ Continental Army won the Battle of Trenton.
   _____ Americans won the Battle of Saratoga.

9. _____ Bill of Rights approved
   _____ Constitution ratified

Boston Massacre

Short Answer

10. What act by Parliament forbade settlements west of the Appalachian Mountains?
_____

11. What British company was given a monopoly on the tea trade in 1773?
_____

12. The Townshend Duties taxed colonists on which imported goods?
_____

13. Who was the king of England during the American Revolution era? _____

14. Which army won the Battle of Brandywine? _____

15. Which act closed the port of Boston? _____

Name: _____ Date: _____

Mercantilism

Until **George III** became king of England in 1760, the colonists had been largely ignored by the king and Parliament of England, mostly because they had been too busy taking care of other matters.

British laws had regulated the government of the colonies from the beginning. For the most part, however, England felt the colonies existed mainly for one purpose—to provide economic benefits for the mother country through trade. They followed a policy called **mercantilism** where they thought a country should sell more goods to another country than it bought.

from England, sent on British ships. Goods **imported** from or exported to other countries were heavily **taxed**, or charged a fee by the government.

In 1760, a new king took over the throne of England. King George III, who ruled Great Britain for 60 years, played an important role in the American Revolution.

The colonists rarely objected at first, because the prices of goods from England were usually less than the cost of the same goods from other countries. Although they lived far away, the colonists considered themselves subjects of England and loyal to the king.

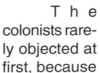

Think About It
Do you think the colonists would have agreed that they existed only for the benefit of the mother country?

The colonists could **export** raw materials only to England and only on British ships. They were also expected to buy goods only

Matching

_____ 1. mercantilism
_____ 2. import
_____ 3. export
_____ 4. King George III
_____ 5. tax

a. shipping goods out of a country
b. a country should sell more goods to another country than it buys
c. a fee charged by the government
d. became ruler of Great Britain in 1760
e. shipping goods into a country

Constructed Response
Explain why England taxed goods imported from or exported to other countries. Give specific details or examples to support your answer.

_____

_____

_____

_____

Consequences of the French and Indian War

The **French and Indian War** lasted from 1756 until 1763. The combined efforts of British troops and American colonists had defeated the French and their Native American allies. As a result, France was forced to give up almost all of her territory in North America.

With French control broken, colonists expected to expand their settlements to the "**West**." At that time, the West meant the area from the Appalachian Mountains to the Mississippi River. However, those hopes were dashed when England passed the **Proclamation of 1763** forbidding any settlements west of the Appalachian Mountains. England had made promises to several native tribes to keep colonists east of the Appalachians. There had also been an uprising in 1763 led by the Ottawa Chief Pontiac during which many settlers' cabins were burned and people were killed. England feared if more settlers moved west, this would cause further uprisings. It would also force England to maintain a large army to keep the peace.

The Proclamation of 1763 angered many colonists who had lived in that area for more than 20 years. Some had been forced to flee during the uprising, but most planned to return to their homes. Thousands of other immigrants planned to move to the new territory once the war ended. Since the colonists had fought with the British against France and they were part of the British Empire, they considered the territory theirs also.

For the most part, the colonists simply ignored the Proclamation of 1763 and continued to move west. Led by **Daniel Boone** and other frontiersmen, settlers moved into western Pennsylvania, Kentucky, Tennessee, Ohio, Indiana, and Illinois.

Although the British Empire was at the height of its power, the country was deeply in debt and needed money to repay loans and rebuild the royal treasury. Since the people in England were already paying high taxes, King George III and the British Parliament decided to raise money by taxing the American colonists. After all, they reasoned, it had cost money for the British government to defend the colonies from the French and Indians, so it was only right that they pay their fair share.

Patrick Henry

The taxes made many of the colonists very angry because they had no representatives in **Parliament** to vote against the taxes or speak for the interests of the colonists. That's what Patrick Henry meant when he said, "Taxation without representation is tyranny."

It would have been difficult for anyone to represent the colonies in Parliament at that time, even if it had been allowed, because of the distance and time it took for messages to travel back and forth by ship. If a representative in England had sent news about a proposed law or tax to the colonies, it would have taken about two months for the news to arrive. Then it would have taken another two months for the colonists to send a reply after they made a decision. By that time, the situation could have changed completely.

Name: _____   Date: _____

Consequences of the French and Indian War (cont.)

Directions: Complete the following activities.

Matching

_____ 1. French and Indian War
_____ 2. the "West"
_____ 3. Proclamation of 1763
_____ 4. Daniel Boone
_____ 5. Parliament

a. lawmaking body of the British government

b. area from the Appalachian Mountains to the Mississippi River

c. led settlers West

d. forbade settlements west of the Appalachian Mountains

e. British soldiers and colonists fought the French and their Native American allies

Fill in the Blanks

1. The French and Indian War lasted from _____ until _____.

2. After the French and Indian War, colonists expected to expand their settlements west from the _____ Mountains to the _____ River.

3. _____ _____ said, "Taxation without representation is tyranny."

4. To rebuild the treasury after the French and Indian War, King George III and the British Parliament decided to _____ the American colonists.

5. The taxes made many of the colonists angry because they had no _____ in Parliament.

Constructed Response

Explain what Patrick Henry meant when he said, "Taxation without representation is tyranny." Give specific details or examples to support your answer.

_____

_____

_____

_____

_____

_____

_____

Name: _____ Date: _____

Expansion of the British Empire

Following the French and Indian War, England acquired much territory in the New World. All of North America north of Spanish-controlled Florida and as far west as the Mississippi River now belonged to England. This included land in Canada formerly controlled by France.

Map Activity

Directions: The area controlled by Great Britain prior to 1763 is shown on the map. Color in the area Great Britain controlled after the French and Indian War.

Name: _____ Date: _____

Taxes on Sugar and Molasses

The **Sugar Act**, passed by Parliament on April 5, 1764, imposed a tax on all molasses and sugar imported by the colonies from the French and Spanish West Indies.

A similar tax, called the **Molasses Act**, had been passed in 1733, but it had been mostly ignored. The colonists refused to pay the tax and simply smuggled the goods into the country. The British government didn't try very hard to enforce the law, either.

However, this time the British were determined to enforce the Sugar Act. They sent inspectors to search warehouses and even pri-

vate residences. The colonists resented paying the taxes and the invasion of their privacy.

The British also offered rewards to citizens who reported anyone smuggling these products. When a smuggler was arrested, the judge who found him guilty also received a reward.

Did You Know?
Molasses from the British West Indies was used by colonists as a sweetener and to make an alcoholic beverage called rum.

Graphic Organizer

Directions: Compare and contrast the Sugar Act and the Molasses Act. Complete the Venn diagram below.

Molasses Act

Sugar Act   Both

UNIT THREE: REVOLUTION & CONSTITUTION

Name: _____   Date: _____

The Stamp Act

It was common in England to raise money by requiring people to buy government stamps for official documents. On March 22, 1765, a similar law went into effect in the colonies. The **Stamp Act** required colonists to pay for a government stamp on newspapers, pamphlets, playing cards, dice, documents, and legal papers, including marriage licenses.

This tax was imposed to raise money to pay the cost for wages and expenses of the 10,000 British soldiers stationed to defend the frontiers against Native American attacks.

Colonists protested that Parliament didn't have the right to tax them because they had no members in Parliament to represent them, a right guaranteed by the British Constitution. **Patrick Henry** gave a speech against taxation without representation. The **Virginia House of Burgesses** declared the Stamp Act illegal and passed resolutions saying England had no right to tax people in Virginia.

In October 1765, delegates from nine colonies met in New York. The group, known as the **Stamp Act Congress**, pledged to resist paying any taxes not approved by their colonial legislatures. Many merchants promised to stop importing British goods. Colonists organized groups like the **Sons of Liberty** whose members felt strongly about unjust taxes.

Angry crowds met the Stamp Masters when they arrived from England to enforce the law. People rioted, destroyed offices, burned the stamps, and forced many Stamp Masters to resign or leave town. The

Stamp Act caused so much dissension that it was repealed a year later. However, Parliament passed a Declaratory Act, which gave them the right to pass laws in the colonies.

Matching

_____ 1. Stamp Act

_____ 2. Patrick Henry

_____ 3. Virginia House of Burgesses

_____ 4. Stamp Act Congress

_____ 5. Sons of Liberty

a. pledged to resist paying any taxes not approved by their colonial legislatures

b. gave a fiery speech against taxes without representation

c. declared the Stamp Act illegal and passed resolutions saying England had no right to tax people in Virginia

d. required colonists to pay for a government stamp on certain paper documents, playing cards, and dice

e. group of colonists who had strong feelings against unjust taxes

Name: _____   Date: _____

The Currency Act and Quartering Act

As businesses grew in the colonies, the **barter** system that had worked before wasn't as effective anymore. People needed money.

Several of the colonies began printing their own money, called **colonial scrip**. British bankers didn't like this, because that meant they might lose control of the American economy.

The **Currency Act of 1764** prohibited the colonies from issuing their own money. It also required colonists to use only British money. When colonists exchanged colonial scrip for British goods or money, their money was worth only half as much.

In essence, this doubled the value of British money and cut the price of goods in half for the British, but had the opposite effect on the colonists. They had to pay double for products.

Unlike most of the other laws **Parliament** passed, this one wasn't designed to raise money through taxes. It was designed to control the American economy.

Another law designed to control the colonists was the **Quartering Act of 1765**. This required the colonists to provide barracks and supplies, including bedding, firewood, cooking utensils, food, and cider, for British troops stationed in the area.

Matching

_____ 1. Currency Act of 1764

_____ 2. colonial scrip

_____ 3. barter

_____ 4. Parliament

_____ 5. Quartering Act of 1765

a. stated that colonists had to provide for feeding and housing British soldiers

b. a system of trading the colonists used instead of money

c. the legislative body of Great Britain, which ruled the colonies

d. money printed by the colonists

e. prohibited the colonies from issuing their own money

Technology in the Classroom
Primary Source: <http://historicaltextarchive.com/sections.php?action=read&artid=650>
("Currency Act, 1764," Don J. Mabry/The Historical Text Archive)

Directions: On September 1, 1764, Parliament passed the Currency Act. This act gave Great Britain control of the colonial currency system. Examine the primary source and summarize the five provisions of the Currency Act on a separate sheet of paper.

Name: _____ Date: _____

The Rebels Unite

Many groups formed to protest the laws and taxes imposed by King George III and Parliament. Some were merely discussion groups. Others were more active.

Sam Adams was one of the first prominent men in Boston to openly favor separation from Great Britain. He formed a secret radical group known as the **Sons of Liberty**. Men in other colonies formed similar organizations. They set up **Committees of Correspondence** to communicate with each other.

After England passed the Stamp Act, Adams recruited more members for the Sons of Liberty and led them in attacks on stamp distributors, customs agents, and other officials loyal to Great Britain.

Sam Adams

Minutemen, groups of local militia who promised to be ready at a minute's notice, secretly prepared to fight the British. They gathered weapons and ammunition and trained as soldiers. When they received **Paul Revere**'s warning, the Minutemen gathered at Lexington to meet the British troops.

Did You Know?

An American Elm tree in Boston Common was a favorite gathering place for protesters against the Stamp Act. The tree soon became known as the Liberty Tree. Straw dummies dressed as British tax collectors were often hung from the limbs of the tree.

Study Aid

Directions: Use reference sources to research the Sons of Liberty, Minutemen, and Committees of Correspondence. Create a study aid to organize the information. Write the names of men who joined the organizations, their goals, and activities inside the front flaps.

1. Fold a sheet of white, unlined paper in half lengthwise like a hotdog bun.

2. Next, fold the paper in thirds, from side to side.

3. Unfold the paper and cut up the front two folds.

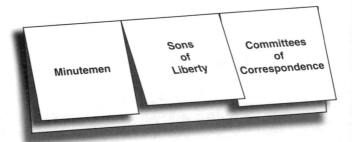

4. On the front of the flaps, write the names of the three groups you researched.

5. Under the flaps, write the information you found about each group.

UNIT THREE: REVOLUTION & CONSTITUTION

Name: _____   Date: _____

More Taxes in 1767

Passed on June 29, 1767, the **Townshend Duties** were taxes on glass, lead, paint, paper, and tea shipped to the colonies. A board of customs commissioners (tax collectors) was sent to Boston.

Mobs in Boston and other towns threatened and harassed tax collectors, who wrote urgent letters to London asking for protection. The colonists also began to **boycott** British goods. The colonists hoped that by boycotting British goods, English merchants would lose so much money that they would complain to Parliament and persuade them to lift the taxes.

General Gage sent troops to Boston in 1768 to protect the customs officials. This caused further problems, more anger, and retaliation on the part of the colonists. The British soldiers wore red coats as part of their uniforms. People who resented the presence of the soldiers called them "Redcoats" and "**Lobsterbacks**," using those terms to make fun of the soldiers.

Again, the British backed down and repealed all of the Townshend Duties on March 5, 1770, except for the tax on tea. On the same day that the Townshend Duties were repealed in England, a mob in Boston attacked British troops. The soldiers killed five people. Colonists called this event the "**Boston Massacre**."

The one good thing that resulted from the Boston Massacre was that British troops were withdrawn from Boston.

Matching

_____ 1. boycott

_____ 2. Boston Massacre

_____ 3. Lobsterbacks

_____ 4. Townshend Duties

_____ 5. General Gage

a. sent troops to Boston in 1768 to protect the customs officials

b. nickname colonists used for British soldiers

c. refuse to buy

d. a mob in Boston attacked British troops, resulting in five colonists being killed

e. taxes on glass, lead, paint, paper, and tea

Technology in the Classroom
Primary Source: <http://www.earlyamerica.com/review/winter96/massacre/massacretext.htm>
("Boston Massacre as reported in the *Boston Gazette*," Boston Massacre Historical Society)

Directions: A detailed account of the Boston Massacre appeared in the *Boston Gazette*. Read the article to find the point of view. Using the perspective of a Loyalist (loyal to the king) or Patriot (wanted American freedom), write a letter to the editor on your own paper voicing your reaction to the article.

Name: _____ Date: _____

Revolutionary Women's Organizations

Sarah Franklin Bache

In 1774, a group of 51 women in Edenton, North Carolina, led by Penelope Barker signed the **Edenton Proclamation**, stating they had a duty to become involved in political issues affecting the colonies. They announced they would not buy tea or English-made clothing. The British believed this was an insult to England.

In 1780, **Esther Reed** began a nationwide drive to raise funds for soldiers. She published a broadside titled "The Sentiments of an American Woman" explaining why women should become involved. In Philadelphia, Esther, along with 36 other women, formed a group called the Association to collect money from other women in the city for soldiers. They raised over $300,000 and served as an example for similar groups in at least seven other colonies. When Reed approached General Washington, he told her it would be better to provide clothing for the soldiers than to give them money that they might spend foolishly.

When Esther Reed died, **Sarah Franklin Bache** took charge. She helped to organize a women's group that used the money to sew linen shirts for the soldiers in the Continental Army. Using her home as headquarters, volunteers made nearly 2,200 shirts. Each was signed by the woman who made it.

Abigail Adams founded the Daughters of Liberty. They met to discuss the political situation and plan ways they could assist in opposing the British. They also contributed their skills at sewing, knitting, and weaving cloth.

Matching

_____ 1. Edenton Proclamation

_____ 2. Esther Reed

_____ 3. Sarah Franklin Bache

_____ 4. Daughters of Liberty

_____ 5. Abigail Adams

a. founded the Daughters of Liberty

b. members met to discuss the political situation and plan ways they could assist in opposing the British

c. stated women had a duty to become involved in political issues affecting the colonies

d. using her home as headquarters, volunteers made nearly 2,200 shirts for soldiers

e. formed the Association to collect money for soldiers

Critical Thinking

Why do you think sewing and making clothing for the soldiers of the Continental Army was an important contribution? Give specific details or examples to support your answer. Write your answer on your own paper.

The Boston Tea Party

The British **East India Company** controlled the tea trade between India, Great Britain, and her colonies. By 1773, this company had a surplus of over 18 million pounds of tea. The tax on tea and the boycotts of British products by colonists had hurt the company.

On May 10, 1773, Parliament passed the **Tea Act**. The law gave a monopoly on tea to the East India Company. A **monopoly** is complete control over a product or service. Only the East India Company could import tea into the colonies. The law also permitted the East India Company to sell tea directly to the colonies through its own agents. Rather than raising the tax on tea, the Tea Act actually lowered it. By lowering the price, it was hoped that the colonists would buy more tea.

It would seem that any law that lowered taxes would be welcomed by the colonists, but that wasn't the case. The first to protest were colonial merchants who had been making money importing tea (sometimes legally, sometimes by smuggling). Other merchants joined the protest. They feared that if Parlia-

ment could grant a monopoly on tea to one company, it might grant monopolies on other products also, putting them out of business. Merchants also stirred up the colonial radicals by claiming this was simply another sneaky way for England to tax the colonists. As a result, crowds rioted in protest.

In December 1773, three British ships carrying East India tea anchored in Boston Harbor. The colonists refused to let the tea come ashore, and the ships refused to leave without unloading. Several thousand colonists complained to the governor, but he refused to listen. In protest of the Tea Tax, about 150 members of the **Sons of Liberty** disguised as Native Americans dumped 340 chests of tea into Boston Harbor on the night of December 16, 1773. This later became known as the **Boston Tea Party**.

Did You Know?
There was another "tea party" in the colonies. At the Yorktown Tea Party on November 17, 1774, two half-chests of tea were thrown into the York River.

Matching

_____ 1. East India Company
_____ 2. Tea Act
_____ 3. monopoly
_____ 4. Sons of Liberty
_____ 5. Boston Tea Party

a. complete control over a product or service
b. protested against the Tea Tax
c. tea dumped in Boston Harbor by Sons of Liberty
d. gave a monopoly on tea to the East India Co.
e. controlled the tea trade between India, Great Britain, and her colonies

Activity

Directions: The colonial tax on tea amounted to about three cents a pound. Find out how much the sales tax is where you live. Compare the tax colonists paid on a pound of tea to the amount you would pay today on a pound of tea.

1. Today's sales tax: _____
2. Today's price for a pound of tea: _____
3. Sales tax on one pound of tea today: _____

Name: _____   Date: _____

The Intolerable Acts

In retaliation for the Boston Tea Party, Parliament passed what the colonists called the **Intolerable Acts**. The Intolerable Acts closed the port of Boston to all shipping. This was to remain in effect until the colonists paid for the dumped tea. The Intolerable Acts also decreased the power of the local authority, the Massachusetts Assembly, and increased the power of royal officials. Only one town meeting would be allowed per year.

To enforce the Intolerable Acts, the British sent General Thomas Gage and regiments of soldiers to Boston. A new **Quartering Act** allowed the British commander to house his troops wherever he wished, even in private homes against the will of the owners.

Although these laws mostly affected those living in Boston, people throughout the colonies protested the Intolerable Acts. The assemblies (local ruling governments) from various colonies sent protests to England in the hope that Parliament would repeal the laws. Again England reacted harshly. More than half the colonial assemblies were suspended.

General Thomas Gage

Graphic Organizer

Directions: Complete the chart below. Write the causes and consequences of each event.

Event	Causes	Consequences
1. Intolerable Acts		
2. Quartering Act		

Name: _____   Date: _____

The First Continental Congress Meets

In protest of the Intolerable Acts, the **First Continental Congress** met in Philadelphia in September 1774. Twelve of the thirteen colonies sent representatives.

Although the idea of freedom from British rule and taxes was a very attractive prospect, winning a war against the mightiest country in the world seemed almost hopeless. Some members of the Congress wanted to break all ties with England. Other members wanted peace with England and tried to persuade the king to repeal the Intolerable Acts. Some members tried to find a compromise that both England and the colonies could agree upon.

After weeks of debate, members of the First Continental Congress agreed to stop all trade with England. If England used force against Massachusetts, they would all resist. They resolved to meet again in May 1775, if the situation did not improve.

While the First Continental Congress met and **debated** the issues, colonists in Massachusetts began arming themselves, forming **militia** groups, and storing gunpowder and weapons. Clashes between colonists and British troops became more frequent.

General Gage, the royal governor of Massachusetts sent to enforce the Intolerable Acts, sent reports to England explaining that the situation was getting much worse. He suggested temporarily suspending the Intolerable Acts and requested an additional 20,000 troops.

Leaders in England thought his reports were exaggerated. They felt he had more than enough troops to put down a few **rebels** in Boston. The king refused to suspend the Intolerable Acts.

Matching

_____ 1. First Continental Congress

_____ 2. debated

_____ 3. militia

_____ 4. General Gage

_____ 5. rebel

a. armed force

b. colonists rising up against the British

c. representatives from 12 of the colonies discussed how to handle problems with Britain

d. discussed

e. governor of Massachusetts

Research

In 1774, 12 of the 13 colonies sent representatives to the First Continental Congress. Research to find out which colony did not send representatives and why.

_____

_____

_____

_____

UNIT THREE: REVOLUTION & CONSTITUTION

The Midnight Ride of Paul Revere

Can a poem change history? Perhaps not, but a good poem or story can change what people believe happened. In 1861, almost 100 years after the event, the poet, **Henry Wadsworth Longfellow**, published "Paul Revere's Ride." Not only was it a very popular poem, it also had the effect of making Paul Revere a national folk hero. The poem begins with these words:

> Listen, my children, and you shall hear,
> Of the midnight ride of Paul Revere,
> On the eighteenth of April, in Seventy-five;
> Hardly a man is now alive
> Who remembers that famous day and year.

Longfellow took an actual event, changed the facts somewhat, and then exaggerated the role played by Paul Revere. The Boston **Committee of Correspondence** employed Paul Revere and others as express riders to carry news, messages, and copies of resolutions to other colonies. On the night of April 18, 1775, they sent Paul Revere from Boston to Lexington to warn Samuel Adams and John Hancock that the British were about to arrest them and to alert the militia that troops planned to seize **munitions**, weapons and ammunition, stored at Concord. They also sent another rider, **William Dawes**, by a different route with the same warning.

That night, Paul Revere instructed Robert Newman and **Captain John Pulling** to place two lanterns in the bell tower of Christ Church in Boston to indicate British troops would be coming "by sea" across the Charles River to Cambridge, rather than marching by land. (One if by land, two if by sea.) After being rowed across the Charles River to Charlestown, Revere met members of the Sons of Liberty to confirm they had seen the prearranged signal.

At Charlestown, Revere borrowed a horse and rode to Lexington, stopping at houses along the way to warn the Minutemen about British plans. He delivered his message to Adams and Hancock around midnight.

Think About It
Why do you think a poet or storyteller would exaggerate the facts used in their writings?

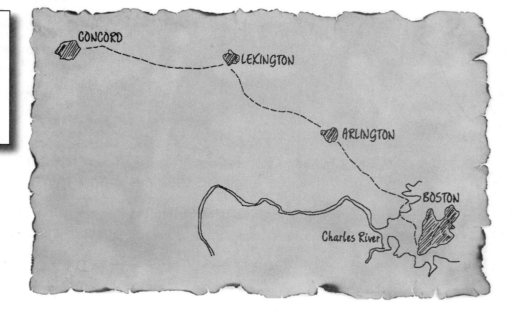

Name: _____   Date: _____

The Midnight Ride of Paul Revere (cont.)

When William Dawes arrived, the two men continued on to Concord to alert the militia to prepare for the British attack. On the way, a third man, **Dr. Samuel Prescott**, joined them.

Before they reached Concord, the three were arrested by a British patrol. Dawes and Prescott escaped, but Dawes was thrown from his horse and couldn't continue. The British held Paul Revere for a time and confiscated his horse. He had to walk back to Lexington. Only Prescott arrived in Concord in time to deliver the warning.

Matching

_____ 1. William Dawes

_____ 2. Dr. Samuel Prescott

_____ 3. Captain John Pulling

_____ 4. Henry Wadsworth Longfellow

_____ 5. Committee of Correspondence

_____ 6. munitions

a. weapons and ammunition
b. employed express riders to carry news to the colonies
c. express rider thrown from his horse and couldn't continue the ride to Concord
d. express rider who warned Concord the British soldiers were coming
e. placed lanterns in the church tower to warn the colonists of Charlestown the British soldiers were coming
f. author of the poem "Paul Revere's Ride"

Graphic Organizer

Directions: Read the poem, "Paul Revere's Ride" by Henry Wadsworth Longfellow. You can find it in most anthologies of American poetry or on the Internet. Use the chart below to compare the events in the poem with what actually happened the night of April 18, 1775.

Inaccuracy in Poem	Actual Historical Event

UNIT THREE: REVOLUTION & CONSTITUTION

Name: _____ Date: _____

Lexington and Concord

On the night of April 18, 1775, colonists in Boston learned the British planned to arrest Samuel Adams and John Hancock and raid the supply depot in Concord. The Boston Committee of Correspondence sent riders to warn Adams and Hancock and to alert the **militia** at Concord of the surprise attack.

When the 600 British soldiers reached Lexington, they found about 80 armed men commanded by Captain Jonas Parker waiting on the village green. The colonists were ordered to put down their weapons and leave. Realizing they were badly outnumbered, Parker ordered his men to disperse, but not to give up their weapons. Suddenly, someone fired a shot. No one knows whether that first shot was fired by a British or colonial soldier. The first shot fired at Lexington has been called "the shot heard 'round the world."

The warning from Prescott gave the people at Concord time to move their weapons and ammunition to safety. News from Lexington arrived before the British. About 400 armed colonials waited for them at a bridge outside Concord. After a short battle, the British commander decided to retreat. The troops began marching back to Boston, a distance of about 16 miles.

At first, the retreat was calm and orderly. Suddenly, musket fire erupted from the woods along the road. Militia units from Lexington, Concord, and other cities had prepared an ambush. The orderly march turned into a **rout**. Nearly 300 British soldiers were killed or wounded. Only the arrival of reinforcements saved them from complete disaster as they continued their hasty retreat to Boston.

Although there had been skirmishes before, Lexington and Concord were considered the first battles of the Revolutionary War. The victory boosted the morale of the colonists. Although they had not yet declared their independence, the **Revolutionary War** had begun.

Matching

_____ 1. rout

_____ 2. militia

_____ 3. Revolutionary War

a. war between the American colonies and Britain

b. armed colonists

c. disorderly, hasty retreat

Fill in the Blanks

1. The first shot fired at _____ has been called "the shot heard 'round the world."

2. The Boston _____ of _____ sent riders to warn Adams and Hancock and to alert the militia at Concord of the surprise attack by the British Regulars.

3. _____ and _____ were considered the first battles of the Revolutionary War

4. When 600 British soldiers reached Lexington, they found about 80 armed men commanded by _____ _____ _____ waiting on the village green.

"Yankee Doodle"

"Yankee Doodle" is a well-known patriotic song from the Revolutionary War played and sung on the Fourth of July to celebrate independence from Great Britain. The melody for "Yankee Doodle" goes back to the 1600s at least, possibly to England or Ireland. British soldiers brought the tune to America and made up new verses to make fun of the colonists. One early version showed how confident the British felt.

Yankee Doodle came to town
For to buy a firelock;
We will tar and feather him
And so we will John Hancock.

The words to the chorus made fun of the men and boys who joined the American army. A "doodle" meant a silly person or a country bumpkin.

Yankee Doodle keep it up,
Yankee Doodle dandy
Mind the music and the step,
And with the girls be handy.

The American soldiers had few weapons, didn't know how to drill, and had little experience fighting battles. They didn't have fine uniforms like the red-coated English soldiers. On April 19, 1775, British troops played "Yankee Doodle" as they marched confidently from Boston to reinforce British soldiers at Lexington and Concord.

"Yankee Doodle" was still being sung when the battle was over, and the Redcoats were forced to retreat back to Boston. On the way back, however, it was colonial soldiers singing "Yankee Doodle," mocking the British as though to say, you might not think much of our abilities, but we'll show you who is a doodle! The song came to symbolize the pride and confidence the colonists felt in their ability to defeat Great Britain.

Constructed Response

Use a dictionary to find the meaning of *dandy*. _____

_____

Why did the British soldiers call the American soldiers dandies? Explain your answer using specific details or examples.

_____

_____

_____

_____

_____

_____

UNIT THREE: REVOLUTION & CONSTITUTION

Name: _____   Date: _____

The Second Continental Congress Meets

Benjamin Franklin

After the battles at Lexington and Concord in April 1775, an informal state of war existed between Great Britain and the colonies. Under the joint command of Ethan Allen and Benedict Arnold, colonial forces captured Fort Ticonderoga. Colonial soldiers also surrounded Boston, keeping British General Gage and his soldiers confined to that area.

Representatives from all 13 colonies hurried to Philadelphia where the **Second Continental Congress** met on May 10, 1775. Patrick Henry and Sam Adams wanted to declare independence immediately, seize British officials, and send for help from France and Spain.

Not everyone in the colonies wanted to go to war against Great Britain, however. For example, even though Benjamin Franklin helped write the Declaration of Independence, his son, William, remained loyal to England.

Even after the **Declaration of Independence** was signed in 1776, announcing to the world that the colonies were independent states and no longer ruled by Britain, opinion was divided. About a third of the colonists, called **Patriots**, wanted independence. Another third were **Loyalists** who did not want to rebel against Britain. The last third were **"fence sitters"**—people who hadn't made up their minds either way.

The majority of the representatives hoped to avoid war. They sent a message to the king saying they didn't plan to separate from Great Britain, but if the British continued to use force, they would resist with force.

Think About It

Why do you think the term "fence sitter" was used to describe colonists who hadn't made up their minds about independence?

Matching

_____ 1. fence sitters

_____ 2. Declaration of Independence

_____ 3. Patriots

_____ 4. Second Continental Congress

_____ 5. Loyalists

a. announced the colonies were independent states

b. colonists who did not want to rebel against Britain

c. meeting of representatives from all 13 colonies

d. colonists who had not made up their minds about independence

e. colonists who wanted independence

Name: _____ Date: _____

The Battle of Bunker Hill

The Second Continental Congress appointed **George Washington** as commander in chief of the Continental Army. If they did go to war, they would need an experienced soldier in charge.

Before Washington reached the main army, General Gage decided to try to break out of Boston by force and teach the colonists a lesson. Hearing of the plan, the American commanders were ordered to fortify **Bunker Hill** on the north side of the city. They made a mistake and dug trenches on **Breed's Hill**, a smaller hill closer to the waterfront.

> **Did You Know?**
> The battle known as Bunker Hill actually took place on Breed's Hill.

The colonists were able to stop the first two attempts by the British to take Breed's Hill, but were forced to flee when troops charged the hill a third time and the colonists ran out of ammunition. Although technically they lost, the battle at Breed's Hill convinced many colonists they could beat the British easily.

The king ordered a **naval blockage** on all the colonies to prevent colonists from receiving supplies. He proclaimed that all the colonies were rebels. Members of the Second Continental Congress recognized that peace with Great Britain might no longer be possible. They sent **ambassadors** to France, Spain, and the Netherlands to request aid.

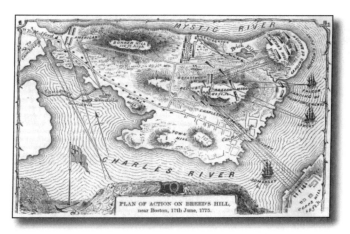

PLAN OF ACTION ON BREED'S HILL, near Boston, 17th June, 1775.

Matching

_____ 1. George Washington

_____ 2. Battle of Bunker Hill

_____ 3. naval blockade

_____ 4. ambassador

a. using ships to cut off supplies and trade to the colonies

b. representative from one country to another

c. really the Battle of Breed's Hill

d. commander in chief of the Continental Army

Constructed Response

Explain why many colonists were convinced they had beaten the British Army at the Battle of Bunker Hill (Breed's Hill). Give specific details or examples to support your answer.

_____

_____

_____

_____

UNIT THREE: REVOLUTION & CONSTITUTION

Name: _____ Date: _____

The Declaration of Independence

War or peace? Debates raged for weeks at the Second Continental Congress. Finally, on June 7, 1776, Richard Henry Lee of Virginia proposed this resolution:

"The United Colonies are, and of right ought to be, free and independent states."

The Congress appointed a committee of five men to write a declaration based on Lee's proposal. Each member of the committee expressed his ideas of what should be included in the document, but the actual writing was left to Thomas Jefferson, a task that took 17 days.

Thomas Jefferson

For three days, members of the Continental Congress discussed the document Jefferson had written. Changes were made. One paragraph in the original that was deleted from the final version had to do with the abolition of slavery. Finally, on July 4, 1776, they voted to adopt the Declaration of Independence.

The Declaration has four major sections.

1. Preamble—tells why the Declaration was being written
2. Lists the natural rights of all people
3. Lists the colonists' complaints against Great Britain
4. States that the 13 colonies are free and independent states

The writers of the Declaration of Independence felt people had certain natural rights that could not be taken away from them. They called these "unalienable rights."

"We hold these truths to be self-evident, that all men are created equal, that they are endowed by their Creator with certain unalienable rights, that among these are Life, Liberty, and the pursuit of Happiness; that to secure these rights, governments are instituted among men, deriving their just powers from the consent of the governed—that whenever any form of Government becomes destructive of these ends, it is the Right of the People to alter or to abolish it, and to institute new Government, ..."

The Continental Congress decided to have an official copy printed in ornamental script on parchment. This was the copy that was signed by 56 members of the Congress on August 2, 1776. When Benjamin Franklin signed his name, he stated, "We must all hang together, or surely we shall all hang separately."

Copies of the Declaration of Independence were printed in Philadelphia and sent to all the colonies. When read out loud in Philadelphia, John Adams reported, "The bells rang all day and almost all night."

Constructed Response

On your own paper, explain what the writers of the Declaration of Independence meant by *unalienable rights*. Give specific details or examples to support your answer.

Name: _____   Date: _____

The Declaration of Independence (cont.)

Research

Directions: Use reference sources to fill in the chart with information about the men selected to write the Declaration of Independence.

Committee Member	Age	Colony	Occupation
Benjamin Franklin	70		Printer, inventor, scientist, diplomat
Thomas Jefferson			Lawyer, inventor
John Adams		Massachusetts	
Roger Sherman	29		
Robert Livingston		New York	

Technology in the Classroom
Primary Source: <http://www.archives.gov/exhibits/charters/declaration_join_the_signers.html>
("The Charters of Freedom," U.S. National Archives & Records Administration)

Directions: Access the primary source website, and click on the "Join the signers of the Declaration" icon. Add your name to a copy of the Declaration of Independence, and print the document.

Study Aid

Directions: The Declaration has four major parts. Create a study aid to help you remember the sections and important information found in each section.

1. Place four sheets of white paper in a stack. Layer the sheets one on top of the other so each has a bottom border of one-half inch showing.
2. Fold the stack of papers in half.
3. Crease the fold and staple across the top.
4. Write the title on the first page and label the tabs Preamble, Rights, Complaints, and 13 States.
5. As you read the Declaration of Independence, write what you learn under the correct tabs.

UNIT THREE: REVOLUTION & CONSTITUTION

The Signers of the Declaration of Independence

Signing the Declaration of Independence was considered an act of treason against the king. If the colonists lost the war, those who signed would likely be hanged.

On July 4, 1776, after two days of debate, the Declaration of Independence was approved by Congress. The actual signing did not occur until August 2, and three men signed it at a later date. Knowing the consequences, these men wrote their signatures on that famous document.

> **Did You Know?**
> Thomas Jefferson was upset by the changes made to the original version of the Declaration of Independence. For years after, he sent copies of both versions to friends asking their opinions of which they liked better.

John Adams
Josiah Bartlett
Charles Carroll
William Ellery
Button Gwinnett
John Hart
Stephen Hopkins
Francis Lee
Thomas Lynch
Robert Morris
Robert Paine
George Ross
James Smith
Matthew Thornton
James Wilson

Samuel Adams
Carter Braxton
Samuel Chase
William Floyd
Lyman Hall
Joseph Hewes
Francis Hopkinson
Richard Henry Lee
Thomas McKean
John Morton
John Penn
Benjamin Rush
Richard Stockton
George Walton
John Witherspoon

Abraham Clark
Benjamin Franklin
John Hancock
Thomas Heyward
Samuel Huntington
Francis Lewis
Arthur Middleton
Thomas Nelson
George Read
Edward Rutledge
Thomas Stone
William Whipple
Oliver Wolcott

George Clymer
Elbridge Gerry
Benjamin Harrison
William Hooper
Thomas Jefferson
Philip Livingston
Lewis Morris
William Paca
Caesar Rodney
Roger Sherman
George Taylor
William Williams
George Wythe

Research

Directions: Research to answer the questions below about the signers of the Declaration.

1. Included among the signers were two future presidents: Who were they?
   _____

2. Who was the first to sign? _____

3. Which of these men was a leading physician of the time and helped found the first American antislavery society? _____

4. Which of these men was later appointed to the U.S. Supreme Court by George Washington?
   _____

5. Born in Gloucester, England, this signer was killed in a duel with Lochlan McIntosh.
   _____

6. This man served as the governor of Virginia from 1782 to 1784. He was the father of one U.S. President and the great-grandfather of another. _____

7. This man was a ship's captain in the African slave trade and later became a merchant in Portsmouth, New Hampshire. _____

Name: _____   Date: _____

The Thirteen Colonies Become States

Directions: Match the names of the 13 original states of the United States of America to the correct numbers on the map.

_____ Georgia   _____ Maryland   _____ Connecticut   _____ Pennsylvania

_____ Virginia   _____ South Carolina   _____ Delaware   _____ New Jersey

_____ Rhode Island   _____ Massachusetts   _____ New York   _____ North Carolina

_____ New Hampshire

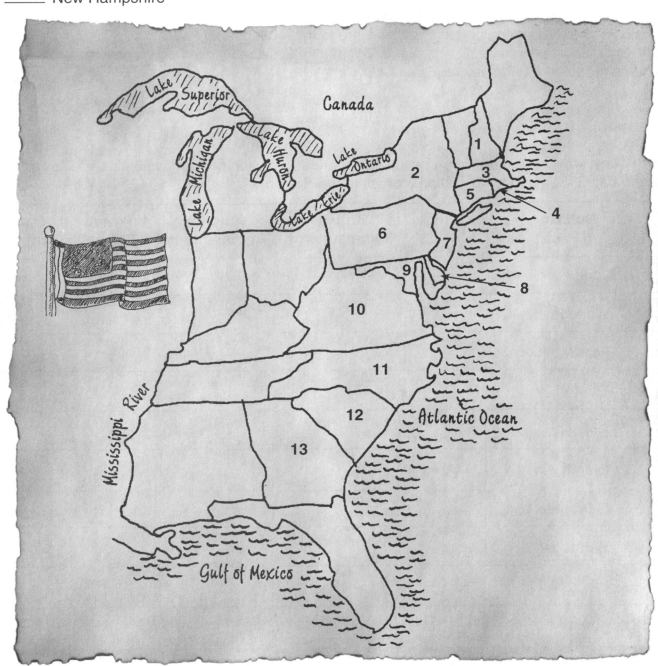

UNIT THREE: REVOLUTION & CONSTITUTION

Name: _____ Date: _____

Battles of the American Revolution

The War of Independence was a costly and lengthy one for both the Americans and Great Britain. Beginning with the battles at Lexington and Concord in April 1775, the war continued until the surrender at Yorktown in October 1781. It was another two years before Great Britain and the United States finally signed a peace treaty.

The Continental Army, under the direction of General Washington, achieved many victories against the British troops. They also suffered many defeats. Battles were fought on land and at sea, as far north as Quebec and Montreal in Canada, and as far south as Pensacola, Florida.

Did You Know?
During the Revolutionary War, more inhabitants of the colonies fought for the British Army than for the Continental Army. Only 16 percent of able-bodied men in the colonies fought in the Continental Army.

Research

Directions: Use reference sources to learn more about each of the Revolutionary War battles listed below. Using the information, complete the chart below.

Battle	Date	British Commander(s)	American Commander(s)	Where Fought	Who Won
1. Long Island					
2. White Plains					
3. Fort Washington					
4. Trenton					
5. Princeton					
6. Brandywine					
7. Germantown					
8. Saratoga					
9. Kings Mountain					
10. Yorktown					

UNIT THREE: REVOLUTION & CONSTITUTION

Name: _____   Date: _____

Patriot or Traitor?

At one time, George Washington called **Benedict Arnold** "the bravest of the brave."

Both Benedict Arnold and Nathan Hale were Revolutionary War heroes. **Nathan Hale**, a schoolmaster, became a captain in the Continental Army. While stationed near New York City, he volunteered to go behind British lines on Long Island to secure vital military information. There he was captured, accused of being a spy, and hanged. To the colonists, Hale was a brave patriot and hero. To the British, Hale was a traitor.

Benedict Arnold led colonial soldiers in several battles against

Nathan Hale's famous last words were, "I only regret that I have but one life to lose for my country."

the British army, but he changed sides in the middle of the war. When Arnold changed sides, the colonials considered him a traitor. To the British, he was a patriot.

Research

Directions: You be the judge. Use reference sources to learn more about the actions of these two men during the Revolutionary War. Create a display for your information like the one below. Write a verdict for each man: patriot or traitor. Explain the reasons for your answers.

1. Fold a white sheet of paper in half vertically.
2. Write Benedict Arnold at the top on one side and Nathan Hale on the other.
3. Add a picture of each man to your display.
4. Use the format below to add your research to the display.

Example:

I think Benedict Arnold was a _____

because _____

_____

_____

_____

The Articles of Confederation

Eight days after the Second Continental Congress approved the Declaration of Independence, John Dickinson presented a proposal for unifying the colonies. This proposal included provisions for a strong central government that would control the western lands, have the power to levy taxes, and allow equal representation for each state.

Dickinson's proposal was not acceptable to most representatives. They feared a central government could become too strong and powerful. If that happened, they would be no better off than they were under British rule.

Changes to the document, which became the **Articles of Confederation**, gave each state as much independence as possible and limited the functions of the **federal** government. As modified, the Articles of Confederation provided for a loose alliance of states with limited powers in a central government.

- The federal government would consist of a **Congress** in which each state had one vote.
- Congress would have the power to set up a postal department, to request donations from the states to cover costs, to raise armed forces, and to control the western territories.
- With consent from 9 of the 13 states, Congress could also coin money, borrow money, declare war, and sign treaties and alliances with other countries.
- Any **amendments** to the Articles of Confederation required the approval of all 13 states.

Even with the changes, it took until March 1, 1781, for all of the states to **ratify** the Articles of Confederation. There were several reasons for the delay.

- Many states were preoccupied with the Revolutionary War.
- Several states quarreled over boundary lines with each other.
- Each state already had its own courts, **tariff** laws, and trade agreements and didn't want to be forced to change.
- Smaller states wanted equal representation with larger ones.
- Larger states feared they would have to pay more than their share to support the federal government.
- The states disagreed about control over the western territories.

Besides not establishing a strong central government, there were several other weaknesses in the Articles of Confederation. Although the Articles of Confederation were weak, they did help hold the new nation together until a stronger document, the United States Constitution, was written in 1787 and approved in 1789.

Name: _____   Date: _____

The Articles of Confederation (cont.)

Directions: Complete the following activities.

Matching

_____ 1. Articles of Confederation

_____ 2. federal

_____ 3. Congress

_____ 4. amendments

_____ 5. ratify

a. approve

b. provided for a loose alliance of states

c. additions or changes

d. national

e. law-making body

Fill in the Blanks

1. The Articles of Confederation provided for a loose alliance of states with _____ powers in a central government.

2. Any amendments added to the Articles of Confederation required the approval of all _____ states.

3. The Second Continental Congress approved the _____ of _____ after changes to John Dickinson's original proposal.

Research

Directions: Research the Articles of Confederation. Complete the chart below by listing the strengths and weaknesses of the government formed under the Articles.

Articles of Confederation	
Strengths	**Weaknesses**

UNIT THREE: REVOLUTION & CONSTITUTION

Name: _____ Date: _____

In Search of Foreign Aid

Declaring independence from Great Britain was a big step, but winning a war against this most powerful country was a near impossibility the colonists could not hope to achieve without outside help.

Members of the **Second Continental Congress** asked 70-year-old Benjamin Franklin to travel to France to request supplies, money, and soldiers from the French king, Louis XIV. They thought France might be willing because of what had happened in 1763 following the French and Indian War.

France had already secretly sent some war materials before Franklin arrived in December 1776. Although the French wanted to see Great Britain defeated by the colonists, they were reluctant to openly form an alliance with the new country in what might be a losing cause. If the colonists didn't win, Britain would probably start another war with France in retaliation.

In December 1777, when Franklin learned about the American victory at **Saratoga**, he repeated his requests. France agreed to sign an **alliance**, but only if Spain would, too. Spain refused because it feared their colonies in Central and South America might also decide to **revolt**. In spite of Spain's refusal, Franklin convinced France to sign an alliance on February 6, 1778. Historians agree that without the soldiers, **naval** support, and millions in cash and goods sent by France, the Americans would have lost the war.

Matching

_____ 1. Second Continental Congress

_____ 2. Saratoga

_____ 3. alliance

_____ 4. revolt

_____ 5. naval

a. stage an uprising

b. pact

c. related to a navy and ships

d. meeting of representatives from all 13 colonies

e. Revolutionary War battle won by the Americans

Constructed Response

Explain why the Second Continental Congress believed France might join them against Great Britain. Use specific details or examples to support your answer.

_____

_____

_____

_____

_____

_____

Name: _____ Date: _____

Surrender at Yorktown

Although he had no orders to do so, Lieutenant General Charles Cornwallis moved his troops north from North Carolina to link up with British forces in Virginia in the summer of 1781. He planned to launch a full-scale offensive against the Continental Army. The British troops drove the Americans, led by the Marquis de Lafayette, out of Virginia.

General Sir Henry Clinton, the commander of British troops in North America, disapproved of this unauthorized action. He sent Cornwallis to establish a defensive position on Chesapeake Bay to **fortify** the towns of Gloucester and Yorktown.

Lafayette sent word about the British position and preparations to General Washington at West Point, New York. When Washington learned that their French **ally**, Admiral de Grasse, was sailing to the Chesapeake Bay area with 29 warships, he set off for Virginia on August 21 with about 7,000 men. They arrived at Williamsburg a month later.

By the time Washington arrived, de Grasse had driven off the British fleet and

General Charles Cornwallis surrenders

blocked Chesapeake Bay, preventing British troops from escaping by sea. De Grasse also provided French troops to reinforce Washington's army.

When the American and French troops arrived at Yorktown on September 28 with a combined force of 16,000, they laid **siege** to the town. Realizing the hopelessness of his position, Cornwallis requested a truce on October 17 and signed articles of surrender two days later. When they learned of the surrender, 7,000 British reinforcements, on their way to Yorktown, returned to New York.

Matching

_____ 1. fortify

_____ 2. ally

_____ 3. siege

a. surrounding and blocking

b. strengthen the defenses

c. friendly nation

Constructed Response

1. It is about 462 miles from West Point to Williamsburg. It took Washington and his troops a month to travel that distance. Averaging 55 miles an hour, how long would it take to drive that far today?

_____

7. If they traveled for 30 days, how many miles a day, on the average, did they march?

_____

The Treaty of Paris

The surrender at Yorktown by General Cornwallis on October 19, 1781, was the last major battle of the Revolutionary War, but the Treaty of Paris, which officially ended the war, was not signed until September 3, 1783.

The most important question to the United States was how much territory they would gain. England agreed to give up all claims in North America as far west as the Mississippi River, except for Canada. (Some colonists also wanted to control Canada to prevent "future difficulties.")

The French were upset when a **preliminary** treaty was signed in November 1782 because they had not been included in the **negotiations**. The United States agreed not to accept the treaty until terms could be reached that would be acceptable not only to France, but also to Spain and the Netherlands (unofficial allies with the colonists).

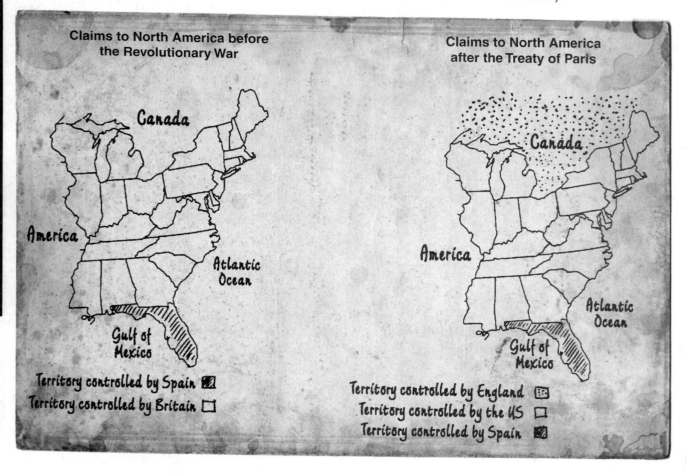

Claims to North America before the Revolutionary War

Canada
America
Atlantic Ocean
Gulf of Mexico

Territory controlled by Spain ▧
Territory controlled by Britain ☐

Claims to North America after the Treaty of Paris

Canada
America
Atlantic Ocean
Gulf of Mexico

Territory controlled by England ▦
Territory controlled by the US ☐
Territory controlled by Spain ▧

Name: _____   Date: _____

The Treaty of Paris (cont.)

In addition to the agreement giving the United States control of more territory, Great Britain also promised to ...

... respect American independence and recognize the former colonies as a free and independent United States of America;

... allow American fishing rights off the Great Banks of Newfoundland and Nova Scotia;

... **relinquish** all claims to government, property, and territorial rights in the former colonies;

... evacuate all British troops;

... return the colony of Florida to Spain;

... return Senegal to France.

The United States agreed to restore the rights and property of Loyalists and allow free movement on the Mississippi River to France, Spain, Great Britain, and the Netherlands.

New York remained the last stronghold of Loyalist support. Beginning in January 1782, thousands of British supporters left the area. Some moved to England; others settled further north in Canada. By December 1783, the last of the British troops had also departed.

The Continental Congress ratified the treaty on January 14, 1784.

> **Think About It**
> Why do you think many Loyalists decided to move after the war, even though the Treaty of Paris promised to restore their rights and properties?

Graphic Organizer

Directions: Complete the vocabulary chart by creating a definition for each word and using each word in a sentence. This will help you remember the meaning of each word.

Word **preliminary**	Definition:
	Sentence:
Word **negotiations**	Definition:
	Sentence:
Word **relinquish**	Definition:
	Sentence:

UNIT THREE: REVOLUTION & CONSTITUTION

Name: _____   Date: _____

Writing the Constitution

After the Revolutionary War, the 13 colonies realized they needed something stronger than the Articles of Confederation to hold them together as a united nation. However, exactly what they needed was a matter of much debate. Only five states sent **delegates** to the first **Constitutional Convention** held in Annapolis, Maryland, in 1786.

All states except Rhode Island sent delegates to the second meeting of the Convention, which was held in Philadelphia the following year. However, it took the delegates four months of debates, arguments, and discussions before they finally made compromises and agreed. On September 17, 1787, 39 delegates signed the final document.

For the Constitution to become official, at least 9 of the 13 states needed to approve it. Although it became effective in July 1788, the last of the original states to **ratify** the Constitution (Rhode Island), did not do so until May 29, 1790.

The **Constitution** is a plan for governing our country. It has three main parts: preamble, seven articles, and the signatures of the signers. The **Preamble** to the Constitution of the United States is the introduction to the document stating the purpose of the Constitution.

We the People of the United States, in order to form a more perfect Union, establish Justice, ensure domestic Tranquility, provide for the common defense, promote the general Welfare, and secure the Blessings of Liberty, to ourselves and our Posterity, do ordain and establish this Constitution for the United States of America.

The rest of the Constitution is divided into **Articles**, or sections, regarding the legislative, judicial, and executive branches of the government, the rights and duties of states and citizens, provisions for new states to enter the union, and describing how the document can be amended.

Matching

_____ 1. Constitutional Convention
_____ 2. delegates
_____ 3. ratify
_____ 4. Constitution
_____ 5. Preamble
_____ 6. Articles

a. sections
b. introduction
c. representatives
d. meeting to revise the Articles of Confederation
e. plan for governing
f. approve

Cooperative Learning

Directions: Working in a small group, examine the Preamble to the Constitution to identify the main idea and key words in each phrase. Using dictionaries and thesauruses, rewrite the Preamble using your own words to express the same ideas. Write the new Preamble across the top of a large sheet of freezer paper or newsprint. Using the paper, create a mural illustrating your Preamble.

UNIT THREE: REVOLUTION & CONSTITUTION

Name: _____ Date: _____

The Bill of Rights

The Constitution was barely a year old when government leaders decided that several guarantees of individual rights needed to be added. In fact, many of the states only ratified the Constitution because they were assured that these protections would be added.

James Madison

James Madison and other members of the Constitutional Convention proposed 12 changes. Ten of these changes, called the **Bill of Rights**, were approved and became a permanent part of the Constitution on December 15, 1791.

The Bill of Rights:

1st Amendment: Guarantees freedom of speech, **press**, religion, and **assembly** (the right to meet peacefully).

2nd Amendment: Protects the right of citizens to bear arms.

3rd and 4th Amendments: Assures the right to privacy and forbids illegal searches of homes.

5th, 6th, 7th, and 8th Amendments: Protects people accused of crimes and provides for trial by a **jury**.

9th and 10th Amendments: Forbids Congress from passing laws that would change the protection guaranteed in the first eight amendments.

When the Bill of Rights was passed, these rights did not apply to everyone in the United States. Women, slaves, and American Indians had no legal rights. Since the Constitution and Bill of Rights were approved and accepted as law by the United States, 17 additional **amendments** have been added.

UNIT THREE: REVOLUTION & CONSTITUTION

Matching

_____ 1. Bill of Rights

_____ 2. press

_____ 3. assembly

_____ 4. jury

_____ 5. amendments

a. the right to meet peacefully

b. a group of people sworn to give a verdict at a trial

c. first ten amendments to the Constitution

d. changes or additions

e. the gathering and publishing or broadcasting of news

Name: _____ Date: _____

Revolutionary Word Search

Directions: Find and circle the 44 words hidden in the puzzle. Words may be printed forward, backward, vertically, horizontally, and diagonally.

```
R L O Y A L I S T S P J M R N N K R N Y V
T E P H I L A D E L P H I A O G L O Y Q K
H B R W T T L R B R T G T I X Z I T G D E
I E E G N X S B H H H T T R E T R S L L C
R R V E O R S O X T G A T L U E M D C M N
T S O N T K E S S Z X R T T B O G L I H A
E E L G G M R T J A E T I I C B F N R S I
E T U L N I G O T A A T L T R A U Y T F L
N A T A I L N N T B S E K I E T P A L C L
J T I N X I O Y Z N T M T T E A O M B U A
D S O D E T C R O O F I D M M C P L A R J
M E N W L I C C V H S D E W D M K A X T Y
X A C J N A C X L H V N H E J M N G R Q S
F V S L Y M B I L L O F R I G H T S L T D
S B B S A S E E K N A Y L A V A N C R V Y
R T L R A R C O N T I N E N T A L A R M Y
O B O O L C A N E C N E D N E P E D N I D
T H G I C M R T C R T D Y O R K T O W N F
I C N Z R K B E I T I Z R M F M H R L R N
A N D M L T A W T O B F M O M M L F A C G
R T K M L D A D K Q N T L Y C H Q N T B H
T T A X E S K P E J Q T W E R N C M Z Q C
D E T I N U S E I N O L O C S E O R Q T Q
N O I T A T N E S E R P E R N J M C K N T
```

RICAN SOLDIER UNDER ARMS. [From a Print of the p

ALLIANCE	DECLARATION	NAVAL	STATES
BATTLE	ENGLAND	PATRIOTS	TAXATION
BILL OF RIGHTS	FRANCE	PHILADELPHIA	TAXES
BLOCKADE	INDEPENDENCE	REBEL	TEA PARTY
BOSTON	JULY FOURTH	REDCOATS	THIRTEEN
BRITISH	LEXINGTON	REPRESENTATION	TRAITOR
COLONIES	LIBERTY	REVOLUTION	TREATY
CONCORD	LOYALISTS	RIFLES	UNITED
CONGRESS	MASSACRE	RIGHTS	VOTE
CONSTITUTION	MILITIA	SIGN	YANKEES
CONTINENTAL ARMY	MINUTEMEN	STAMP ACT	YORKTOWN

Patriots

Research

Directions: Learn more about one of the people on the list below. Using this information, fill in the blanks on the bookmark. On the other side of the bookmark, create an illustration that represents the important contribution the person made to the Revolutionary War era. Cut out the bookmark. Punch a hole at the top, run yarn through the hole, and tie.

Abigail Adams
John Adams
Samuel Adams
Ethan Allen
Benedict Arnold
Crispus Attucks
Sarah Franklin Bache
Penelope Barker
David Bushnell
George Rogers Clark
Lydia Darragh
John Dickinson
Benjamin Franklin
Mary Katherine Goddard
Nathanael Greene
Nathan Hale
Alexander Hamilton
John Hancock
Patrick Henry

Stephen Hopkins
John Jay
Thomas Jefferson
John Paul Jones
Marquis de Lafayette
Charles Lee
James Monroe
Francis Marion
Thomas Paine
Mary Hays (Molly Pitcher)
Esther Reed
Paul Revere
Betsy Ross
Deborah Sampson
Mercy Otis Warren
George Washington
Martha Washington
Anthony Wayne
Phillis Wheatley

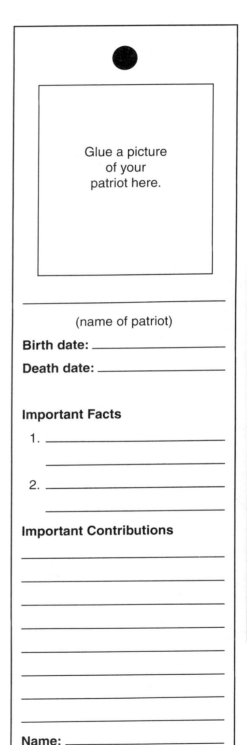

Glue a picture of your patriot here.

_____
(name of patriot)

Birth date: _____

Death date: _____

Important Facts

1. _____
   _____

2. _____
   _____

Important Contributions

_____
_____
_____
_____
_____
_____
_____
_____
_____

Name: _____

UNIT THREE: REVOLUTION & CONSTITUTION

Mercy Otis Warren

Francis Marion

Answer Keys

Unit One: Discovery and Exploration of the Americas
(No answers are listed for activities where answers may vary.)

Time Line Activity (p. 2)
1. 1541
2. fountain of youth
3. 1496
4. about 985 A.D.
5. Honduras
6. Hernan Cortés
7. Mississippi River to the Gulf of Mexico
8. 1526
9. Vasco Balboa
10. about 1000
11. 1513
12. 1530
13. Sebastian Cabot
14. 1499–1512
15. 1536
16. southeastern United States
17. Hudson Bay
18. 1492–1502
19. Samuel de Champlain
20. 1497

Land Bridge Theory (p. 3)
Matching
1. c   2. a   3. b   4. d

Viking Exploration (p. 4)
Technology in the Classroom
1. They both were buried with their property.
2. 25–60 crew members
3. Runes were used as writing symbols, for fortune-telling, casting spells, and protection.
4. hnefatfl (king's table)
5. knorr or knarr

Leif the Lucky (p. 6)
Matching
1. c   2. e   3. a   4. b
5. d
Fill in the Blanks
1. three, Red
2. Greenland's
3. Christianity
4. lack, trees
5. Leif, Lucky

The Lands of the Vikings (p. 7)
Teacher check map.

Christopher Columbus (p. 9)
Matching
1. b   2. c   3. a   4. e
5. d
Fill in the Blanks
1. Atlantic Ocean
2. Ferdinand, Isabella, Spain
3. Asia, land
4. San Salvador
5. East Indies, Indians
Constructed Response
Columbus was looking for a sea route to China that would be shorter and safer than traveling by land. He thought he could do this by sailing west.

The Four Voyages of Columbus (p. 10)
Teacher check map.

Vasco Nuñez de Balboa (p. 13)
Matching
1. f   2. b   3. h   4. e
5. c   6. g   7. d   8. a
Fill in the Blanks
1. New World
2. gold
3. Panama
4. Native Americans
5. Pacific Ocean
Constructed Response
Balboa believed it was better to have the native people as friendly neighbors rather than bitter enemies. One example is that he hired guides on his expedition across Panama. When they couldn't go any farther, he rewarded them and hired other guides.

Trade With the Far East (p. 14)
1. Africa
2. To find a water route to India
3. Many of the crew died from scurvy. They encountered many fierce storms and had several battles along the east coast of Africa with Muslim traders who did not want the Portuguese to interfere with their trade.
4. The voyage took over two years. They left Lisbon in July 1497, and returned in September 1499.
5. One could reach India by sailing west around Africa

Amerigo Vespucci (p. 16)
Matching
1. d   2. e   3. b   4. c
5. a
Fill in the Blanks
1. Italian
2. Mars, moon
3. Portuguese
4. Tierra del Fuego
5. captain
Multiple Choice
1. d   2. b   3. a   4. c

John Cabot (p. 18)
Matching
1. a   2. e   3. d   4. b
5. c
Fill in the Blanks
1. west, east
2. Henry, England
3. Lewis, Sebastian, Sancio
4. Matthew
5. fish
Constructed Response
They could sail to all parts, regions, and coasts of the eastern, western, and northern seas. They were given the rights to find, discover, and investigate whatsoever islands, countries, regions, or provinces of heathens and infidels in whatsoever part of the world placed, which before this time were unknown to all Christians.

Sebastian Cabot (p. 20)
Matching
1. b   2. e   3. a   4. c
5. d
Fill in the Blanks
1. North America
2. water passageway
3. spice
4. abusing, disobeying
5. northern, China

Magellan Circumnavigates the Earth (p. 21)
1. To sail or fly completely around the earth
2. He believed he could find a passage to India through or around South America.
3. Magellan was killed in a battle on Cebu Island.
4. South America, Asia, Africa, Europe
5. The earth is round.

Juan Ponce de León (p. 23)
Matching
1. c   2. a   3. e   4. b
5. d
Fill in the Blanks
1. page
2. Columbus
3. knighted, governor
4. Florida
5. fountain, youth

Hernan Cortés (p. 26)
Matching
1. d   2. e   3. b   4. c
5. a
Fill in the Blanks
1. Veracruz
2. Quetzalcoatl
3. Montezuma
4. Mexico City
5. Baja California

Francisco Pizarro (p. 28)
Matching
1. e   2. a   3. d   4. c
5. b
Fill in the Blanks
1. Vacso, Balboa
2. gold
3. ransom
4. native
5. assassinated
Constructed Response
Pizarro was cruel and destructive to the Incas. He invited them to a feast, then had his soldiers slaughter them. He took Atahualpa hostage, promised he would let him go when the ransom was paid, and then executed him. He looted the cities, and tortured, killed, and enslaved thousands of Incas.

Francisco Vasquez de Coronado (p. 30)
Map Activity
A. California   B. Arizona
C. New Mexico   D. Texas
E. Kansas   F. Arkansas
G. Oklahoma

Hernando de Soto (p. 32)
Matching
1. e   2. a   3. d   4. b
5. c
Fill in the Blanks
1. Francisco Pizarro
2. South America
3. stealing, villages
4. Europeans
5. river, natives
Graphic Organizer
Francisco Pizarro: was second-in-command; helped to lure Inca emperor into a trap and take him hostage
Native Americans: had their crops stolen, villages burned, and were enslaved
His men: died of sickness, in attacks, and from insect and snake bites; they urged de Soto to return home, but he refused
King Charles: appointed de Soto governor of Cuba and Florida; didn't trust de Soto and Pizarro together

Jacques Cartier (p. 34)
Matching
1. a   2. d   3. b   4. c
5. e
Fill in the Blanks
1. North, Pacific
2. Atlantic
3. *Canada*
4. Saguenay
5. leader
Graphic Organizer
Cartier's Accomplishments: crossed the Atlantic in half the normal time on his first voyage; claimed land for France
Cartier's Failures: did not find the promised passageway; many of his men died; did not bring riches back to the king

Samuel de Champlain (p. 36)
Matching
1. d   2. e   3. c   4. b
5. a
Fill in the Blanks
1. navigation, mapmaking
2. fur trading
3. Quebec
4. Lake Champlain
5. governor

Henry Hudson (p. 38)
Matching
1. b   2. a   3. e   4. c
5. d
Fill in the Blanks
1. England
2. Far East
3. Russia
4. Dutch
5. mutinied

René Robert Cavelier, sieur de La Salle (p. 40)
Matching
1. e   2. b   3. d   4. c
5. a
Fill in the Blanks
1. Ohio
2. forts
3. Louisiana
4. France
5. mutinied
Graphic Organizer
Purposes of Exploration: hoped to find a water passage across the continent; to establish a colony at the mouth of the Mississippi River
Obstacles He Had to Overcome: two ships sank, one was captured, and one returned to France, leaving the colonists stranded without supplies; many died from diseases, rattlesnake bites, and attacks by natives; his men mutinied
His Accomplishments: discovered the Ohio River; established forts; claimed land for France; named Louisiana; Viceroy of North America; Commander of Fort Frontenac in charge of the fur trade

Searching for the Explorers (p. 41)

1. O   2. E   3. N   4. F
5. K   6. G   7. I   8. C
9. M   10. B   11. J   12. H
13. L   14. D   15. A

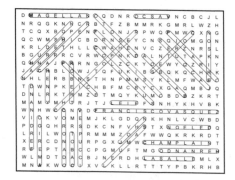

Where Were the Explorers Born? (p. 42)

1. Balboa   Spain
2. J. Cabot   Italy
3. S. Cabot   Italy
4. Cartier   France
5. Champlain   France
6. Columbus   Italy
7. Coronado   Spain
8. Cortés   Spain
9. de Soto   Spain
10. da Gama   Portugal
11. Hudson   England
12. La Salle   France
13. de León   Spain
14. Magellan   Portugal
15. Pizarro   Spain
16. Vespucci   Italy

Unit Two: Life in the Colonies

Time Line Activity (p. 46)

1. 1776
2. tea
3. Benjamin Franklin
4. 1633
5. 1718
6. French and Indian
7. 1775
8. *The Whole Booke of Psalmes*
9. slavery
10. 1607
11. c   12. c   13. d   14. b
15. a

The Original Thirteen Colonies (p. 49)

1. E   2. H   3. M   4. I
5. A   6. B   7. F   8. C
9. K   10. G   11. D   12. L
13. J

New England Colonies:
     Connecticut, Massachusetts,
     New Hampshire, Rhode Island
Middle Colonies: Delaware, New
     Jersey, New York, Pennsylvania
Southern Colonies: Georgia,
     Maryland, North Carolina,
     South Carolina, Virginia

The Kitchen (p. 50)

1. M   2. B   3. C   4. C
5. B   6. C   7. M   8. C
9. M   10. B   11. B   12. B
13. M   14. C   15. M

Colonial Tools (p. 54)

1. H   2. C   3. D   4. A
5. G   6. I   7. B   8. E
9. F

Learning About New Foods (p. 55)

1. Am   2. Am   3. Am
4. As   5. As   6. Am
7. As   8. Am   9. Am
10. As   11. As   12. E
13. Am   14. E   15. As
16. E   17. E   18. Am
19. E   20. As

Soapmaking (p. 59)
Fill in the Blanks

1. lye, water
2. tallow
3. ashes
4. burns, lungs, poisonous
5. soft soap

Cabinetmakers (p. 69)
Research

1. A lathe is a machine that spins a piece of wood, so the woodworker can cut into it with a chisel or other tool to cut grooves and make rounded shapes in the wood.
2. It is used to make rounded pieces like table legs or chair spindles.

Wheelwrights (p. 70)
Diagram

A. iron ring   B. rim
C. spoke   D. hub

Pewterers and Silversmiths (p. 72)
Graphic Organizer

Pewterers: worked with pewter
Both: considered artisans; use hot metal poured into molds; produced shoe buckles, buttons, candleholders, dishes, spoons, cups, teapots
Silversmiths: worked with gold, brass, copper, and silver

Colonial Word Search (p. 78)

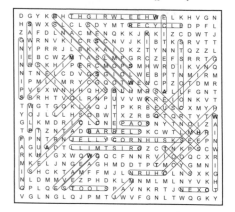

Unit Three: American Revolution

Time Line Activity (p. 82)

1. George III became King of England
2. Currency Act prevented colonists from issuing their own money
3. Boston Massacre
4. Battles fought at Lexington and Concord
5. Declaration of Independence approved
6. British surrendered at Yorktown
7. Stamp Act repealed
8. Continental Army won Battle of Trenton
9. Constitution ratified
10. Proclamation of 1763
11. British East India Company
12. glass, paper, and tea
13. George III
14. British Army
15. Intolerable Acts

Mercantilism (p. 83)
Matching
1. b   2. e   3. a   4. d
5. c
Constructed Response
Great Britain followed a policy of mercantilism. Britain felt the colonies existed mainly for one purpose—to provide economic benefits for the mother country through trade. By taxing imported and exported goods, Britain was forcing the colonists to trade only with Britain.

Consequences of the French and Indian War (p. 85)
Matching
1. e   2. b   3. d   4. c
5. a
Fill in the Blanks
1. 1756, 1763
2. Appalachian, Mississippi
3. Patrick Henry
4. tax
5. representation
Constructed Response
King George III and Parliament decided to raise money to pay for the French and Indian War by taxing the American colonists. The taxes made many of the colonists angry because they had no representatives in Parliament to vote against the taxes or speak for the interests of the colonists.

Expansion of the British Empire (p. 86)
All the territory north of Florida and west to the Mississippi River should be shaded.

Taxes on Sugar and Molasses (p. 87)
Sugar Act: passed in 1764; smugglers arrested; Britain sent inspectors to search warehouses and private residences
Both: passed by Parliament; caused smuggling; tax on sugar and molasses
Molasses: passed in 1733; ignored by colonists; not enforced by British

The Stamp Act (p. 88)
Matching
1. d   2. b   3. c   4. a
5. e

The Currency and Quartering Acts (p. 89)
Matching
1. e   2. d   3. b   4. c
5. a

More Taxes in 1767 (p. 91)
Matching
1. c   2. d   3. b   4. e
5. a

Revolutionary Women's Organizations (p. 92)
Matching
1. c   2. e   3. d   4. b
5. a

The Boston Tea Party (p. 93)
Matching
1. e   2. d   3. a   4. b
5. c

The Intolerable Acts (p. 94)
Graphic Organizer
1. Causes: retaliation for the Boston Tea Party
Consequences: closed Boston Harbor to all shipping until the colonists paid for the dumped tea; decreased the power of the Massachusetts Assembly; increased the power of royal officials; only one town meeting a year was allowed
2. Causes: to enforce the Intolerable Acts
Consequences: British sent General Thomas Gage and regiments of soldiers to Boston; colonists had to house the soldiers

The First Continental Congress (p. 95)
Matching
1. c   2. d   3. a   4. e
5. b
Research
Georgia was the newest and smallest province and declined to send a delegation because it was seeking help from Britain to protect colonists from attacks by the Creek tribe.

The Midnight Ride of Paul Revere (p. 97)
Matching
1. c   2. d   3. e   4. f
5. b   6. a

Lexington and Concord (p. 98)
Matching
1. c   2. b   3. a
Fill in the Blanks
1. Lexington
2. Committee, Correspondence
3. Lexington, Concord
4. Captain Jonas Parker

"Yankee Doodle" (p. 99)
Constructed Response
A *dandy* is a man who is overly concerned with his clothes and appearance. The British were making fun of the colonists by calling them dandies. The colonists did not have uniforms. The British soldiers had red-colored coats.

The Second Continental Congress Meets (p. 100)
Matching
1. d   2. a   3. e   4. c
5. b

The Battle of Bunker Hill (p. 101)
Matching
1. d   2. c   3. a   4. b
Constructed Response
The colonists were able to stop the first two attempts by the British to take Breed's Hill. They were forced to flee when troops charged the hill a third time and the colonists ran out of ammunition. This convinced many colonists that they could beat the British easily.

The Declaration of Independence (p. 102–103)
Constructed Response
People had certain natural rights that could not be taken away from them, including the right to life, liberty, and the pursuit of happiness.

Research
1. Pennsylvania
2. 33, Virginia
3. 40, lawyer and teacher
4. Connecticut, lawyer and judge
5. 55, lawyer

The Signers of the Declaration of Independence (p. 104)
1. John Adams and Thomas Jefferson
2. John Hancock
3. Benjamin Rush
4. Samuel Chase
5. Button Gwinnett
6. Benjamin Harrison
7. William Whipple

The Thirteen Colonies Become States (p. 105)
13. Georgia
10. Virginia
4. Rhode Island
1. New Hampshire
9. Maryland
12. South Carolina
3. Massachusetts
5. Connecticut
8. Delaware
2. New York
6. Pennsylvania
7. New Jersey
11. North Carolina

Battles of the American Revolution (p. 106)
1. Aug. 27, 1776; William Howe; George Washington; New York; British
2. Oct. 28, 1776; William Howe; George Washington; New York; British
3. Nov. 16, 1776; William Howe; George Washington; New York; British
4. Dec. 25–26, 1776; Johann Rall; George Washington; New Jersey; Americans
5. Jan. 3, 1777; Charles Mawhood; George Washington, Hugh Mercer, and Major Samuel Nicholas; New Jersey; Americans

6. Sept. 11, 1777; William Howe; George Washington; Pennsylvania; British
7. Oct. 4, 1777; William Howe, Charles Cornwallis, Wilhelm von Knyphausen; George Washington, Nathanael Greene; Pennsylvania; British
8. Sept. 19 and Oct. 17, 1777; John Burgoyne, Simon Fraser, F.A. Riedesel, Johann Specht, Wilhelm R. von Gall; Horatio Gates, Benedict Arnold, Benjamin Lincoln, Enoch Poor, Ebenezer Learned, Daniel Morgan; New York; 1st battle: British; 2nd battle: Americans
9. Oct. 7, 1780; Patrick Ferguson; Colonel William Campbell (chosen as the leader by the other colonels); North and South Carolina; Americans
10. Sept. 28–Oct. 19, 1781; Charles Cornwallis, Charles O'Hara; Comte de Rochambeau, Comte de Grasse, George Washington; Virginia; Americans

The Articles of Confederation (p. 109)
Matching
1. b   2. d   3. e   4. c
5. a
Fill in the Blanks
1. limited
2. 13
4. Articles, Confederation
Research
Strengths: power to set up a postal department; estimate the costs of the government and request donations from the states; raise armed forces; control the development of the western territories; coin, borrow, or appropriate money; declare war and enter into treaties and alliances with foreign nations

Weaknesses: Congress had no power to collect taxes, regulate trade, or enforce laws; no single leader or group directed government policy; no national court system; could not pass laws without the approval of 9 states; could not change the Articles without the agreement of all 13 states

In Search of Foreign Aid (p. 110)
Matching
1. d   2. e   3. b   4. a
5. c
Constructed Response
Great Britain won the French and Indian War and forced France to give up almost all claims to land in North America in Canada and east of the Mississippi River.

Surrender at Yorktown (p. 111)
Matching
1. b   2. c   3. a
Constructed Response
1. Slightly less than eight and a half hours
2. 15.4 miles per day

Writing the Constitution (p. 114)
Matching
1. d   2. c   3. f   4. e
5. b   6. a

The Bill of Rights (p. 115)
Matching
1. c   2. e   3. a   4. b
5. d

Revolutionary Word Search (p. 116)

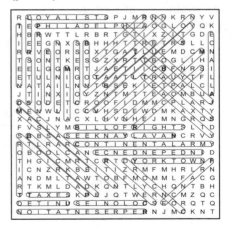